Building the Right Team

Building the Right Team

Maximizing Human Resources

Louis J. Pepe

ASB ASSOCIATION OF
SCHOOL BUSINESS OFFICIALS
INTERNATIONAL

ROWMAN & LITTLEFIELD
Lanham • Boulder • New York • London

Published by Rowman & Littlefield
An imprint of The Rowman & Littlefield Publishing Group, Inc.
4501 Forbes Boulevard, Suite 200, Lanham, Maryland 20706
www.rowman.com

6 Tinworth Street, London SE11 5AL, United Kingdom

British Library Cataloguing in Publication Information Available

Library of Congress Cataloging-in-Publication Data

Names: Pepe, Louis J., author.
Title: Building the right team : maximizing human resources / Louis J. Pepe.
Description: Lanham : Rowman & Littlefield, [2021] | Includes bibliographical references. | Summary: "With relevant anecdotes and a fresh perspective, this book provides leaders a path to getting the best out of their leadership team"—Provided by publisher.
Identifiers: LCCN 2021009880 (print) | LCCN 2021009881 (ebook) | ISBN 9781475854480 (cloth) | ISBN 9781475854497 (paperback) | ISBN 9781475854503 (epub)
Subjects: LCSH: Teams in the workplace. | Leadership. | Personnel management.
Classification: LCC HD66 .P426 2021 (print) | LCC HD66 (ebook) | DDC 658.4/022—dc23
LC record available at https://lccn.loc.gov/2021009880
LC ebook record available at https://lccn.loc.gov/2021009881

Contents

Contents

When we put others ahead of ourselves we are called altruistic.
When we put the needs of the team ahead of our own we are called leaders.

This book is dedicated to my brother Bernd Landau, an accomplished professional who epitomized what it meant to be part of a team and continuously demonstrated his ability to build, manage and lead teams effectively through commitment, skill and grace.

To say I miss him is an understatement; however, recognizing him through this book memorializes his gift for building teams and ensuring their success through his leadership.

Foreword

Siobhán McMahon

I have been fortunate to work with many incredible leaders throughout my career, and especially as a member of the leadership team of the Association of School Business Officials (ASBO) International.

One exemplary leader—a former school business official—empowered me with words I carry to this day: "Surround yourself with people who are more skilled than you are—then get out of their way," "Make sure your folks have the tools they need to get the job done," and my favorite, "I have you on this team to say 'no' to me." He knew how to build a high-performing team, establish a truly open-door policy, and establish an environment in which everyone is valued.

Lou Pepe is another one of those leaders who has made an impression on me, so when he asked me to write the Foreword for his book about leadership teams, I was honored. I have seen firsthand that Lou walks the leadership talk. A longtime member of ASBO International, he has contributed extensively to his school district, the association, and the school business profession through publications, presentations, and leadership on national and state committees. Recently, he was recognized with the ASBO International Eagle Award, the association's most prestigious honor.

So, when he shared a couple of years ago that he was writing a series of books based on his Reality-Based Leadership© framework, I knew the books would be something every leader would want—and need—on their bookshelf.

In this, his fourth book in the series, Lou shares expertise gained over a thirty-year career, providing a unique perspective that challenges leaders to think about their roles and responsibilities in building and leading teams. Entertaining and informative, he once again demonstrates his expertise in masterful team building, offering clear guidance and actionable steps throughout the book that readers can implement straight away.

After taking readers through the process of identifying, attracting, and selecting high-quality team members, Lou breaks down the essential leadership skills required to deliver a high-performing team, from ensuring members have the necessary tools to grow and be effective to rewarding individual performance, boosting team performance, and unleashing the team's potential.

Lou does not shy away from providing insight into the more challenging sides of leading a team—what he calls "the tougher side of HR"—including delivering honest and critical feedback to allow for growth and suggesting someone leave the team to be successful elsewhere. With relevant anecdotes and a fresh perspective, Lou provides leaders a path to getting the best out of their team.

With a candid, sincere, and welcoming writing style, Lou provides valuable advice for all of us who serve in a leadership capacity no matter the industry or profession, regardless of whether we are seasoned leaders or new to team building. It is a book for every leader—and team—intent on improving their processes and their outcomes!

Lou emphasizes the responsibility and expectations of the leadership role, writing, "When we fail to act, we fail to lead. When we fail to lead, we lose the trust and respect of those on the team who are doing the right thing and expect us to make the tough decisions we get paid to make." Yet, he makes the leadership role seem not so lonely, always brings us back to the underlying thread of the book: "Relationships are at the heart of teaming, and that is what strengthens our teams."

We all know that the leader sets the tone and the expectations of the team. This book will help you be that exemplary leader. A leader whose words and actions not only push a team or organization forward—but leave an indelible mark on those around you. It is an essential addition to your leadership library.

Siobhán McMahon, CAE
Chief Operations Officer
ASBO International—Ashburn, VA

Preface

Teamwork is the ability to work together toward a common vision. The ability to direct individual accomplishments toward organizational objectives. It is the fuel that allows common people to attain uncommon results.

—Andrew Carnegie

Reality Based Leadership (RBL)© A conceptual framework of common sense!

Louis J. Pepe, CFO, MBA, RSBA, SFO

The RBL series is written based on my thirty years of management experience in building, managing, and leading teams to achieve desired outcomes while completing tasks, implementing strategies, and accomplishing goals. This is necessary in any organization to accomplish the ultimate objective—the mission.

Each book is meant to provide a glimpse into differing facets of organizational management that allows for continued success through refinement of skills promoting operational awareness in today's rapidly evolving world of business.

Teams are what allow us to achieve great things, greater than any one individual, greater than any one victory. The iconic basketball star Michael Jordan, who played fifteen seasons in the NBA, winning six championships with the Chicago Bulls, put it best when he said, "Talent wins games, but teamwork and intelligence win championships." Teams are the vehicle that carries us to our destination in achieving our vision, our mission, and our goals.

TOGETHER—EACH—ACTION— MAGNIFIES—STRENGTH

Teams are indispensable in all aspects of *planning* and *problem solving*—provided they are effective, well constructed, and ready for action. Successful organizations and companies are staffed with teams that continuously rise to any challenge they are met with. They are full of individuals who are properly trained, equipped, and complete with the right stuff. The stuff that legends are made of are integrity, tenacity, creativity, loyalty, bravery, and ingenuity. They are the lifeblood of organizations; they are the *difference makers* that enable those organizations to flourish or cause those organizations to fail.

They are what lies at the core of any organization's ability to meet the challenges they face—*successful teams* are ones in which leadership is encouraged, expected, and demanded. They are known for their *trust, value,* and *high expectations.*

Great organizations and great companies, like any successful professional athletic team, expect membership within the organization or company to be earned, maintained, and results oriented. In the Pros, when individuals stop producing or lose value for the organization they are traded, retired or let go—either way they are off the team. Sounds harsh, but that is reality and in many private organizations that reality is what maintains order, discipline, and longevity; however, in public sector organizations and private companies that deal with union labor, that reality is fraught with challenges to disciplinary action, transfers and termination under the safety measures of seniority, tenure rights, and grievances.

Unions are important because they help set the standards for education, skill levels, wages, working conditions, and quality of life for workers. They are also important in shaping and supporting legislation that guards against wrongful termination, whistleblowing, and other discriminatory actions that absent such protections would allow management in bad companies to trample the rights of workers. But that's is not what this book is about—it's about working together despite the challenges that are always in play, that can pit labor and management against the ultimate goal of harmony and progress. Having spent years on both sides of the table in a number of organizations both public and private, I have learned one inescapable fact—teams depend on everyone working together to achieve success (figure 0.1).

The Germans have a saying, "All beginnings are hard." (Proverbial meaning: Anything worthwhile takes time and effort.) No matter what you are undertaking in life, whether it's building a company from the ground up, embarking on a career, or leading a team in working on a project, if you start something from scratch, you need the strength of a team to succeed in achieving great feats. Building those teams requires thought, determination, and perseverance to identify and acquire talent and then find ways to transform that talent into groups that work together towards a common purpose—one of strength, one of achievement, one of success.

The subject matter in this book is not just advice for the reader, it is tried and true evidence of success through teamwork and failure when teams break down. It underscores the challenge of teambuilding through the role of Human Resources in order to strengthen our ability as leaders to achieve lasting success on a large scale.

Over a thirty-plus-year career in leadership, team building, and managing people, this is something that I have worked to master and continue to seek improvements whenever and wherever possible. That's how important it is and it requires a deep appreciation for the value of teamwork.

> We can be. We believe in each other . . . that's everything. We are going to do great things. It's an experience—love, tragedy, joy . . . it's something that people will feel belongs to them.—RAMI MALEK— Freddie Mercury

I have found that the best leaders are those who believe in the team as more than just a concept but instead see it as a necessity to the fulfillment of achievement.

Louis J. Pepe
Lincoln Park, 2021.

Acknowledgments

Special thanks to my editors:
Tom Koerner, Senior Editor and
Carlie Wall, Managing Editor
And
My proofreader
Jeannine Dotten
And
The teams I have been a part of and those I have built
along with the many talented professionals I have been blessed to connect
with in my networks over the past thirty years
across two contents, four major industries, and countless fields.

Part I

GATHERING TALENT

Chapter 1

The Strength of the TEAM

For the strength of the pack is the wolf, and the strength of the wolf is the pack.

—Rudyard Kipling, *The Jungle Book*

Teams have been in existence since the beginning of time as soon as two or more gathered to work together in pursuit of accomplishing something that alone was not possible. Clans and tribes, for example, worked together as teams to meet the basic needs of safety and survival in ways that the individual could not. Together they learned that teamwork increased their strength and effectiveness at hunting, gathering, and defending their families within the clan or tribe—the earliest form of communal living.

The Romans understood and valued the strength of the team concept and applied it to build an empire. *"Strength and Honor"* was the creed by which the Romans built a civilization and managed an empire for 500-plus years (27 BC–476 AD). It became the watchword for their greatest teams: the legions that defended Rome and her borders and conquered new lands; and the senate who governed the empire stretching from Spain in the West to the Caspian Sea of Asia Minor in the East and from Britannia in the North to Egypt in the South encircling the Mediterranean Sea at the height of their success in 117 AD.

In the movie *Gladiator* the motto, "Strength and Honor," was used by Maximus, general of the Felix Legions, which was not just a catchy phrase to motivate his troops but was the personal code of the real Emperor Marcus

Aurelius, as well as the Roman army. The soldiers on that day took an oath to support the emperor. In essence, they pledged their lives to him. Their life's purpose—their duty—was to serve. To fail in this duty was to disgrace themselves. The soldiers literally lived and died by this honor code. To a person of honor, "A life without it was not worth living."[1]

When it comes to building teams, Disney gets it right! Their popular inspirational movies are filled with examples of the *strength of the team*—how teams work, why they are needed, and the importance of building and maintaining them.

- *The Jungle Book*[2]—Demonstrates the strength of the individual (Mowgli) and how his strength becomes amplified through the strength of the team (the wolf pack) since the group gains as much from him as he gains from them.
- *Remember the Titans*[3]—Proves that attitude reflects leadership and how acquiring the right attitude can overcome differences to transform us into teams that can be invincible.
- Invincible[4]—Teaches us how determination, perseverance, and spirit can triumph over adversity and become infectious. It reminds us no matter how many times we are knocked down we must rise—and together as a team, we become stronger for the effort.

While these are clearly movies to inspire, teach, and entertain us—they are well thought out and relevant to our need for stronger teams in our own pursuit of success for our organizations. Make no mistake, Disney is a business, an American diversified multinational mass media and entertainment conglomerate headquartered at the Walt Disney Studios complex in Burbank, California, which trades on the Nasdaq under the stock symbol (DIS) currently trading at $131.75,[5] a share with a net worth of $238.08 billion as of September 11, 2020.[6]

Anyone who has had the privilege of working with Disney and their leadership group understands quickly how the power of a story can work in any business or organization to build and strengthen teams that become more effective, productive, and profitable. In 2010 I had the fortune of attending a seminar in Orlando prepared and presented by the Disney Institute regarding Disney's Approach to People Management on communicating and nurturing the culture of the workplace. This remains vital to the successful management of our employees. The presenters explored proven techniques used to select, train, retain, and communicate with employees. That was ten years ago, and the need has only increased! Seminars like this one allow leaders to engage in relevant business applications and take away ideas and best practices to implement in their own organizations.

In a recent blog, Bruce Jones, senior cast development director of Disney Institute writes, "One of the key leadership lessons we have learned from Walt Disney centers around the importance of building relationships with employees and colleagues." After all, it was Walt who once said, "You can design and create, and build the most wonderful place in the world. But it takes people to make the dream a reality."

> Walt's people-management skills were essential to helping him achieve his vision, and he believed a successful leader must maintain healthy relationships.[7]

Relationships are at the heart of teaming and that is what strengthens our teams along with adequate training, properly outfitting them, and effective leadership with clear direction and focus. When people feel connected they get engaged, when they feel valued they contribute, and when they feel appreciated they work harder—but at the heart of any team is a sense of belonging.

No one wants to be left out, and yes, that's a thing! It has been since we were kids trying to fit into groups and social circles, from what we watched on TV, to the clothes we wore and what bands or singers we liked and disliked to what professional sports teams we followed. Even those who deviated from the crowd still belonged to the conversations as they were following someone or some team who belonged to a group and therefore the conversation.

> Teamwork relies on camaraderie, so teams need to be given the space to find common ground and to get to know one another properly if they are to forge deeper and longer lasting relationships.
>
> Being connected, respected and having that all important sense of belonging unites team members around their purpose as they strive to deliver. In turn, purposeful and meaningful work breeds ownership, engagement, accountability and commitment to the team and the organization.[8]

Nowadays, with social media in the form of friending/unfriending with Facebook, following or, better yet, being followed on Twitter, or building connections on LinkedIn, we continue that quest to belong. This continues into our adult lives and, as such, carries forward into our working environments.

Regardless of how secure individuals may be—we all like being liked and more importantly, being accepted and recognized as belonging to teams in our personal, social, and professional lives.

Who doesn't like being selected for an important assignment based on their recognized knowledge and skill set? Often times this means temporary teams that carry opportunity for further recognition within our company, organization, or field. It provides a stage for showcasing that talent by sharing what you know, think, and can figure out in problem-solving while at the same time learning from others based on their knowledge and skill set.

Through our associations, efforts, and experiences, we build connections and therefore contacts. Better yet is when those contacts actually like you and you like them—that's a bonus! And it is that connection that drives us to seek acceptance and join successful teams.

Staying connected is what keeps individuals front on mind when the opportunity to build teams emerges, and once again, those connections stand a much better chance of being selected to participate on yet more teams. But keep in mind while it is nice to like and enjoy the company of others on our teams, our teams need to be effective and able to produce the desired outcomes sought, or the team will be dismantled and or see individuals removed from those teams or like we use to say, "Kicked off the team!"

> The most effective teamwork happens when individual contributors harmonize their efforts and work toward a common goal.[9]

Disney's approach to managing people and communication through story was so impressive that we later brought them to New Jersey to present at our own state conference for School Business Administrators in 2013. A few years later, while serving as Immediate Past President, I was thrilled to have Vince Papale come to share his experiences in 2015 as a former player with the Philadelphia Eagles and give us insights behind the making of *Invincible* based on his story, which has become another Disney blockbuster that has grossed $58.5 million[10] since its release in 2006. *Remember the Titans* has grossed $136.7 million[11] since its release in 2000.

Each of these films recognizes the *strength that teams possess* and why they are important to the overall success of organizations. The National

Research Council of the National Academies backed up this statement in their research release in 2015 *Enhancing the Effectiveness of Team Science*, stating, "Team composition and assembly involve putting together the right set of individuals with relevant expertise to accomplish the team goals and tasks and to maximize team effectiveness."[12]

Strong teams help businesses and organizations achieve goals and outcomes that are uncommon—without them (strong teams) we would see mediocre results, resulting in short-lived companies or long-standing companies beginning to die. Teamwork is the ability of individuals to work together through a shared commitment and vision. Leading those teams allows great leaders to direct individual accomplishment toward organizational objectives. It is the energy that powers the attainment of goals and delivers results that are rare in other companies or organizations. Channeling that effort is where great leaders stand out as great coaches. That is what is necessary and that is what is typically found in successful companies and organizations that flourish and continue to grow.

Creating and maintaining strong teams is vital to any company or organization's future and absent that strength may lead to sluggish returns, stock devaluation, or loss of sales that can lead to filing for Chapter 7, 11, or 13 bankruptcies.

> Inevitably, people will disagree and something will need to change, even on high-performance teams. However, if a business can lead its teams to find solutions rather than further discord, making it through the tough times (and learning from them) is more likely to lead to success than insolvency.[13]

Teams simply can't survive in an environment of contention, frustration, selfishness, and uncertainty. It's still possible to turn a team like this around, but only if cooperation, teamwork, and true leadership become the team's true values once again.

Here is one example from *Teams That Failed to Stay Afloat (And What Sank Them)*[14]

1) LA Lakers—Basketball organization (NBA)—cause: Personnel clashes, ineffective leadership, and high turnover:

> Let's face it: Shaquille O'Neal and Kobe Bryant never hit it off. After the LA Lakers won three straight NBA championships from 2000–2002, these two uncompromising, Type-A players were paired up—and the team was never the same.

Unfortunately, the strained pairing was just the beginning of the LA Lakers' slow demise. Bad trades were negotiated and good ones fell through. Players got injured and then healed too slowly. Coach clashes and backlashes took place over and over again. All of these situations resulted in a high turnover of both players and coaches.[15]

Another example of how poor management of teams added to a company in trouble can be found with the fashion retailer Forever 21:

2) Forever 21—Retailer (malls)—cause: Falling sales further impacted by significant employee dissatisfaction:

Landing at # 7 in the Top 10 of *The Worst Companies to Work For*[16] in a Special Report by 24/7 Wall St., LLC, a Delaware corporation which runs financial news and opinion over the Internet, found a fractured team framework within the many challenges experienced by the retailer: "Forever 21 is a retailer with about 600 U.S. locations, many of which are located in malls, and 35,000 employees. The company claims it is the fifth largest specialty retailer in the country. Forever 21 employees reviewing the company on Glassdoor complain of a too-small employee discount, low pay, and extremely high expectations from managers. Just 30% of those submitting reviews approve of the management style of company founder and CEO Don Chang."[17]

By October of 2019, it had been reported that the brand was embroiled in more than fifty lawsuits involving celebrities, luxury brands, union groups, its own employees, and independent designers.[18]

These examples serve to underscore the importance of teams and treating them right, which is a critical step in making them great teams—back to "*attitude reflects leadership*"—no matter how talented your team members are, they will not perform to their highest capabilities if they feel they are being mistreated. It's all about perception, and in this case, perception is reality. If you fail to recognize how they perceive their treatment, you will soon realize the same troubles that befell both of these organizations.

So how do we avoid these pitfalls and what should we be looking for in creating strong teams? We need to develop characteristics that make teams great by ensuring they are high functioning (productive), high achieving (effective), and operating under a shared vision (common goals). In order to

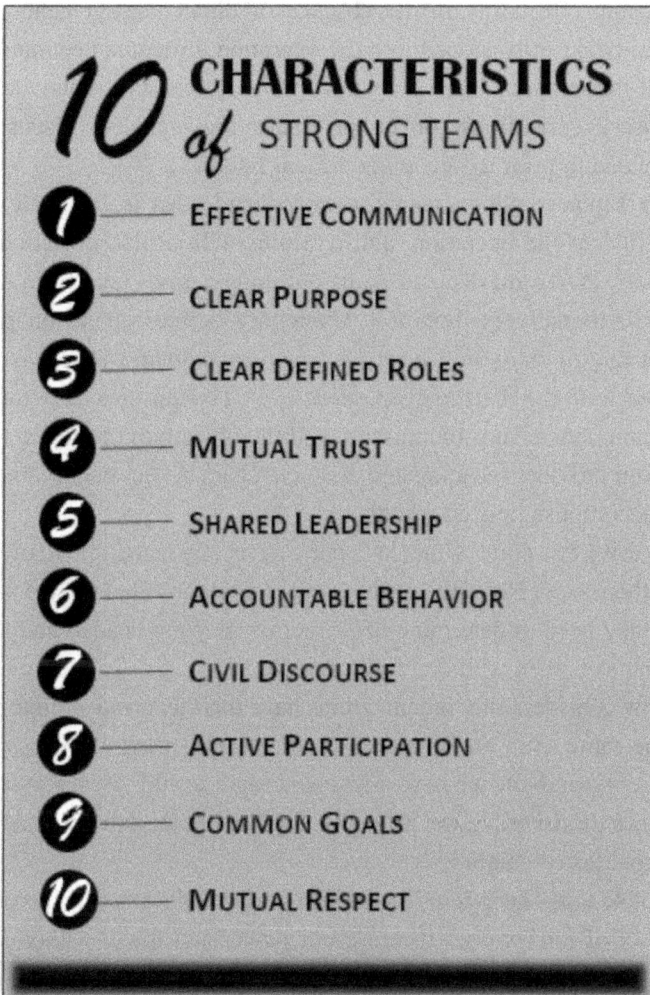

10 CHARACTERISTICS *of* STRONG TEAMS

1 — EFFECTIVE COMMUNICATION

2 — CLEAR PURPOSE

3 — CLEAR DEFINED ROLES

4 — MUTUAL TRUST

5 — SHARED LEADERSHIP

6 — ACCOUNTABLE BEHAVIOR

7 — CIVIL DISCOURSE

8 — ACTIVE PARTICIPATION

9 — COMMON GOALS

10 — MUTUAL RESPECT

Figure 1.1   **Ten Characteristics of Strong Teams**. *Source*: Self-created.

master this, you should focus on these ten characteristics that are inherent to strong teams (figure 1.1).

1. **Effective Communication**—Any team that intends on accomplishing great things needs to communicate openly and honestly up and down the chain of command. This ensures all members of the team know *what* is happening, *what* is expected, and *why* they are doing what they are doing when called upon to act and, more importantly, to be able to continue

producing effectively in the absence of direct management—in other words, being truly looped into the operation through a keen understanding of the mission. Open lines of communication ensure any deviations, necessary corrections, or minor issues are signaled, discussed, and responded to prior to becoming critical issues.

2. **Clear Purpose** allows teams to understand what is expected and how they fit into the operation, and it begins with a plan of action (POA). In short, POAs are detailed plans outlining actions needed to reach our goals. Alternatively, Business Dictionary defines an action plan as a *"sequence of steps that must be taken, or activities that must be performed well, for a strategy to succeed."*[19] This ensures each member of the team understands the mission and the objectives of the organization. Purpose provides meaning and, as such, channels our energy into actions that accomplish desired results.

    To drive this point home, let's put a team, any team, into a rowboat and give them oars. Not only do they need to get those oars in the water, but first they need to determine the direction they are headed and then start pulling as a team with one fluid motion.

    Now consider other organizations have their teams in similar rowboats on the same river, and they too are intent on getting to the same places as your team. Now we have a race and logic would say, the more rowers we have on our team, the more powerful our team will be, thus reaching our goal faster—right?

    Not so fast—keep in mind the role purpose plays; while increasing the number of rowers does increase our power and force, without purpose, teams push and pull in all directions resulting in struggle, fatigue, and discord and actually go nowhere.

    Purpose drives us individually and joins us as a team—it gets us rowing in the same direction and allows us to get where we need to go. It is that simple.

3. **Clear Defined Roles** allow our teams to accomplish goals and objectives in the quickest, most efficient way without stepping on each other, thus avoiding duplication of effort. Likewise, it ensures tasks are completed versus being forgotten, avoided, or overlooked by assuming someone else was going to take care of it or presuming it falls under someone else's job.

The other half of "roles" is "responsibilities" that's why the heading "roles and responsibilities" finds itself on job descriptions to ensure this is understood by the individual and the supervisor; however, this understanding is made stronger when the group understands each role and responsibility in the work of the team. Again I call on the words of Francis Bacon, "Knowledge is power."[20] This is easy to do; however often ignored—strong teams meet frequently to discuss what's happening now, what's coming, and what are the challenges. This provides an opportunity to check on who is doing what and what is expected of everyone. By doing this as a team, we strengthen our understanding of roles and responsibilities and also provide authority to those involved in the tasks as not to be challenged by others on the team.

4. **Mutual Trust**—Trust is everything! When we trust people, we give of ourselves freely and without fear of negative consequences. When we trust our people and they trust us, we act as one team with one aim, to accomplish our goals together and as a team, achieve success that we can all celebrate. Our outcomes are better, effective, and lasting. Absent that trust we experience doubt and suspicion, which leads to holdups, trepidation, and constant challenges. These negative consequences lead to weak and ineffective teams that produce weak or ineffective results—just the opposite of what we seek to accomplish with goals and objectives.

5. **Shared Leadership** shares the burden and gives license to those in our charge to display knowledge, guidance, and skill in troubleshooting and assist others on the team as needed. It provides a framework of cooperation, assistance, and combined strength. This allows for administrative support in completing tasks assigned and ensures support of managerial resources, thus freeing up managers and supervisors to administrate the effort.

In a post from CollectivePossibilities,[21] a boutique consultancy that works with individuals and teams to bring about a shift in thinking that engages minds and enhances capability, the group informs us that *shared leadership* is about empowering people to take leadership positions in their areas of expertise by moving outside of more formalized structures that can inhibit shared contribution. They provide the following points to consider when embracing this practice:

- *Delegate power to the most qualified individuals in the team to strengthen their capabilities*

- *Define the limits of decision-making power—be sure people know where they can and cannot influence decisions*
- *Cultivate a climate in which people feel free to take initiative on projects—encourage responsible risk taking*
- *Give qualified people discretion and autonomy over their tasks and resources and encourage them to use these tools*
- *Don't second guess the decisions of those you have empowered to make them—trust your people*
- *Consider yourself a resource rather than the manager*[22]

6. **Accountable Behavior** ensures all members of the team are tied to their actions while operating as members of the team, whether they are in charge or on the front line of the effort. Accountability is what makes each of us answerable to the mission. Our actions should always be direct toward the benefit of the organization and in keeping with the standards set forth by the organization to include a code of ethics. This comprises moral standards and accountability that encompasses the individual and the group. It is never the wrong time to do the right thing and strong teams not only understand this concept—they live by it.

7. **Civil Discourse** requires tact, respect, and civility. It permits freedom to express one's view along with their ideas even if they are different or not in line with those of the leader; however, it should always be conducted based on team improvement. Isolated issues involving individual performance or personal conflict should be dealt with in private with the team leader and or supervisors.

   Often teams struggle with how and when to engage in discourse (verbal interchange of ideas[23]) without compromising the teams' effectiveness or disrupting a team's cohesive relationship. It can be pretty tricky since many aspects of leadership such as *chain of command, urgency, safety, security,* and *authority* seem to be less than inviting to questioning the directions, orders, or practices team members engage in or are expected to carry out. These identified aspects are in place for a reason and as such require strong adherence to ensure teams operate effectively and without fail in times of crisis as well as regular operations when expected outcomes are directly linked to accountability of those in charge. So how do we reconcile this quandary? Can we promote an environment where civil discourse is permitted and disagreements are not suppressed or overridden by premature group action?

The answer is yes; however, the solution hinges on other elements of strong teams discussed earlier such as trust, leadership, and accountability governed by timing, opportunity, and need.

Leaders have a higher degree of accountability, and no one wants to be second guessed when leading a team. In a crisis or state of emergency, such action could be life threating along with insubordinate. But during times of planning, professional development, or debriefing after an exercise—questions, comments, and observations should be welcomed and considered to find ways to improve performance of those teams in future actions.

Taking other opinions into consideration is not a sign of weak leadership; it is actually the opposite. Strong teams led by strong leaders are leaders who are self-assured and confident in their own abilities and therefore more receptive and willing to hear other perspectives. However, in the end, those leaders are in charge, and by virtue of the chain of command, they are authorized and expected to make the final decision. While that decision is final and rests with them, so do the consequences of those decisions.

Timing determines whether or not we can stop to discuss alternatives. Stressful environments such as crisis management place our teams on a tighter degree of immediacy to act as time is of the essence and clearly limit the ability for group discussion as teams must react quickly to the threat before them.

Teams that seek to resolve differences rather than dominate the dissenter are better at achieving differences of opinion. In situations where disagreements cannot be resolved, strong teams figure ways to work it out and coexist while supporting the final decision(s). This preserves the trust and maintains the respect necessary to carry on and achieve even greater success in the future.

8. **Active Participation** is easily identified in strong teams as every member is engaged in team activities and operations. They don't just show up, but they show up ready to do their part and see the tasks as important to the overall success rather than work. They take pride in what they do, how they look, and what they represent—the organization. In the military, it is referred to as Esprit de corps, a feeling of pride, fellowship, and common loyalty shared by the members of the team or larger group. Most

important, they recognize the importance of each person's contributions and understand the larger burden to the group when they are not there to perform their task.

9. **Common Goals** strengthen teams by providing unity in a cause that goes beyond purpose. While *purpose* gives us the reason, resolve, and determination (our why), *cause* gives rise to our actions (our what) based on a deep commitment to something we are prepared to defend or advocate. When people or groups are committed to a cause, they become unstoppable as they seek an aim for which their actions are carried out in furtherance of achieving it. Common goals bring teams together as they all become invested in the same outcomes.

10. **Mutual Respect** keeps teams strong, honest, and held in high regard. With more generations than ever working together in organizations that are becoming increasingly more diverse, encouraging this characteristic will aid in reducing workplace stress and increase productivity:

    - "Reduce workplace stress, conflict and problems. An increase in workplace respect will help to improve communication between colleagues, increase teamwork and reduce stress as peace in the workplace soars."[24]
    - "Increase productivity, knowledge and understanding. As mutual understanding and respect increase, the exchange of ideas will rise, which will increase company knowledge and innovation. Reducing the amount of pettiness and workplace politics will also assist in increasing productivity. The goal will shift from one-upping a colleague to focusing on the company as a whole."[25]

    Respect is universally sought, expected, and needed for teams to become strong and then required to stay strong; achieving such respect begins with management as they set the tone. The old adage to get it, one must give it seems to apply quite nicely here, and the reality is once it is given, it is generally appreciated and reciprocated.

Chapter 2

Attracting Talent

"Square One"—attracting talent. This is where teambuilding begins and this is where teambuilding matters most. Each time we hire, we are adding individuals (ingredients) to the mix of the culture that exists within our companies or organizations. Hiring is not just a task; it is a critical function of team building that shapes our teams moving forward. We all talk about people being irreplaceable when they are great, and the truth is there never will be another Michael Jordan in the NBA or John Elway in the NFL.

Jordan won six championships in two spells with the Bulls between 1984 and 1998. He had a comeback in the early 2000s with the Wizards, but it's MJ's five-time MVP career with the Bulls—especially his final season—that's become the subject of a lengthy documentary produced by Netflix and ESPN.

But the fact remains—teams win championships, "Even the great Michael Jordan needed some help to win championships."[1]

Jordan had many teammates that assisted in propelling the Bulls to the playoffs and beyond; of course, he had the constant assistance of two superstars in their own right, Dennis Rodman and Scottie Pippen. "Scottie was probably the absolute perfect player to play alongside MJ, and huge credits to the Bulls organization for drafting him. Without Scottie, the Bulls might not have won all six championships. It's very telling that the only player on all six championship teams, besides MJ, is Scottie."[2]

Jordon's quest for championships was not based on self-recognition or the need to have the spotlight focused on him—it was about a commitment to the Chicago organization and the fans and *ultimately about the team*. In an early interview about his career expectations, he responded, "I just want the franchise, and [the] Chicago Bulls, to be respected as a team."[3]

Considered by some to be the greatest modern American football player, John Elway played in the position of quarterback for the Denver Broncos for sixteen years, leading his team to two consecutive Super Bowl wins before retiring in 1999.

Like Jordan, Elway was not alone in accomplishing great feats that led to the Super Bowl wins in 1997 and 1998. He was surrounded by teammates that posted incredible stats and earned many a trip to the Pro Bowl and two players, Shannon Sharpe and Terrell Davis, spots in the NFL Hall of Fame. Davis rushed for 157 yards and a Super Bowl–record three touchdowns to earn the Super Bowl Most Valuable Player Award.

They were truly gifted players who shaped teams that went on to win championships. But the fact is there are always other individuals with the skill, determination, talent, and drive to move teams forward—you just have to *find them*, *develop them*, and *lead them*. If this were not true, we would never have heard of Jason Kidd, LeBron James, or Kobe Bryant or seen players like Drew Brees, Aaron Rodgers, or Peyton Manning. This is the heart of leadership development and it starts with hiring. But as great as each of these superstars are as individuals, they are and were *part of a team*, and it is the *team* that allowed and continues to allow each of them to thrive.

It's amazing to see companies or organizations be sparing with Human Resources in the hiring process. Instead, they should put as much time and effort into each staffing decision as the Pros do to acquire the same degree of talent to lead and support their organizations in achieving their goals.

When it comes to building a team, the most important decision for your team is who are we taking? As children, we use to pick sides for everything we did—capture the flag, kick ball, whiffle ball, touch football (which always turned into *tackle and pummel* in my neighborhood), and other activities that needed quality players to win. Being picked meant you perform better or the next time around at "the choosing" you were guaranteed to go last—and nobody wanted to be there. We were young, fearless, and unsupervised. God, I miss those days! But truth be told, there were leaders among us who emerged and organized the play, the game selected, and the sides with captains. What we didn't realize is just how organized we actually were and how much leadership impacted our outcomes.

Years later, I think about the *draft* in professional sports and how the simple process we used as kids has taken on such importance and value in terms of preparation and compensation depending on where someone is chosen by round and pick number—and trust me they don't want to go last either.

If you ever watched the process for the NFL, you'd witness the immediate excitement and intensity matched with adrenaline that goes into achieving the selections for various teams. Being "on the clock" only adds to the suspense while the commissioner awaits the selection from representatives of the thirty-two teams that make up the league.

Now think about staffing teams within your own organization. Having the ability to pick from the "best of the best" is what every HR director dreams of, or should be dreaming of, if they wish to contribute and remain vital to the organization in their own right.

"In the early years of the draft, players were chosen based on hearsay, print media, or other rudimentary evidence of ability. In the 1940s, some franchises began employing full-time scouts. The ensuing success of these teams eventually forced the other franchises to also hire scouts."[4] In order to increase our chances of hiring the best of the best, we need to look at strategies and techniques for increasing not only *the size of our pools* but *the quality of candidates* within those pools.

This includes scouting of our own or as the military refers to it—reconnaissance. The days of running an ad in the local paper and interviewing four to six candidates who meet the requirements on paper are over for most, if not all, companies and organizations intent on succeeding in the highly competitive Professional World of Business (PWB).

Every organization and business owner should put as much time, effort, and money into the hiring process as the Pros do since it is the biggest investment in their future—bar none.

This starts with attracting more talent to broaden our pools *(larger [targeted] talent pools)* and then *strengthening those pools* by ensuring the talented candidates in the pool are representative of the quality we need in our organizations to benefit our teams (figure 2.1).

ATTRACTING TALENT		STRENGTHENING POOLS
Improve Job Postings	**1**	Improve Job Postings
Shorter Time to Hire	**2**	Simplify the Process
Use of Social Media	**3**	Use of Social Media
Employee Referral Program	**4**	Employee Referral Program
Employee-led Recruiting	**5**	Maintain Active Contacts
Brand Utilization	**6**	Professional Associations
Campus Recruiting	**7**	Retiree Recruiting

Figure 2.1   Seven Techniques and Strategies for Attracting Talent and Strengthening Candidate Pools. *Source*: Self-created.

SEVEN TECHNIQUES AND STRATEGIES FOR ATTRACTING TALENT AND STRENGTHENING CANDIDATE POOLS

1. **Improve Job Postings**—An effective job posting is one which attracts great talent into the pool thus strengthening the pool. The number of *qualified candidates* is what matters most as we are typically hiring for one position within each pool. Our goal should be to create larger pools; however, we need to focus on ensuring *quality* over *quantity* within our pools. This starts by *crafting* a job posting that evokes interest from the ideal candidates. The best place to be in a hiring decision is where you have multiple standouts to choose from versus taking the best of the bunch. That's settling, and truth be told, we have all done it at some point in our career and learned the hard way.

Stocking our pool with an abundance of quality candidates begins with defining the elements of the job (the necessities) while capturing the essence of the opportunity (the perks) you are providing. This is why you should be *crafting versus drafting* job postings to allure and secure the right person before someone else gets them—lest we forget about the rules of *supply and demand.*

Today, there are many web-based solutions providing applicant tracking software for managing the hiring process by managing candidate information and providing valuable tools throughout the process. One such company TalentLyft headquartered in Zagreb, Croatia, is helping companies build awesome teams and grow by assisting recruiters and HR professionals who are looking to hasten, streamline, and ease their recruiting and hiring strategies. They recognize that "job seekers look for clarity in the job advertisements in terms of the profile, company history, pay scale, and career opportunities. A smart recruiter provides a clear picture of every required detail in the job notification. You should be able to clearly communicate job requirements and how one can benefit from this profile."[5]

The takeaway here is simple—*the more time you put into developing an accurate and informative job posting, the better your applicant pool will look.* This not only attracts talent; it strengthens the pool of quality candidates that match the skill set you are looking for in the job. The focus should be quality over quantity, and an effective job posting will cut down on unqualified applicants, thus saving time and energy in the process.

2. **Shorten Time to Hire/Simplify the Process—By** shortening the *time to hire* and *simplifying the process,* we achieve both our aims of attracting talent and strengthening our pools as we become more advantageous to job seekers (a bird in the hand), especially the talented ones who view us as "having our act together"—knowing what we want and committed to getting it.

This does not mean to rush the process—by all means, you need to ensure due diligence in screening, conducting multiple interviews (depending on the importance of the job), and proper vetting. That is to be expected if you want to guard against bad hires; however, the process needs to be completed in the shortest amount of time possible as opposed to dragging it out beyond average time to hire within your industry. In construction, that's around two weeks (avg. 12.7 days),[6] whereas the time to hire in education is closer to a month (avg. 29.3).[7]

According to LinkedIn's 2017 global survey,[8] hiring takes anywhere from a few days to four months. *Time to hire* can be used interchangeably with *time to fill*; however, *time to fill* captures the time for the entire hiring process, from job requisition to job acceptance; whereas, *time to hire* captures the time the eventual hire entered the talent pipeline to the time they accept the offer of employment. "This means your *time to hire* timeline begins when your best candidate applies or gets sourced. This metric shows you how quickly your hiring team was able to identify the best candidate."[9] This is especially important when selecting a recruiter or working with a search firm. You want to ensure you are acquiring a recruiter that knows not only how to scout talent but how to acquire that talent quickly before your competition lands them.

3. **Use of Social Media** has become an effective tool in both *attracting talent* and *strengthening our pools* due to its ease, quickness, and lower cost as an effective option to traditional print ads. "One of the best options that social media platforms give recruiters is the ability to live recruit new employees. Screening employees has never been so simple because of the possibilities that social media offers when interviews and testing are concerned."[10]

Beyond that, social media allows you to get at the newest members of the labor pool in ways that meet them where they live, online. With social networking sites like Facebook, Twitter, LinkedIn, and Instagram, it's a wonder why anybody is still checking the want ads. Add to this, online jobsites that specialize in filling the need for professional organizations like Glassdoor, CareerBuilders, ZipRecruiter, theMuse, and Indeed, and you're hard pressed to refute the fact-based evidence that times have changed and social media is here to stay for the foreseeable future in the world of staffing.

4. **Employee Referral Programs** work in tandem to achieve our desired results of attracting talent and lead into employee-led recruiting. When we bring someone into the fold, we carry a personal responsibility to ensure their success. We become invested in their success and often go out of our way to ensure that success.

Nobody wants to get burned, and that's exactly what happens when you put your reputation on the line to vouch for someone's character, skill set, and overall value to the organization. "Internal referrals result in better hiring outcomes. Research has found that referred candidates are of higher quality than applicants from the general public and are more likely both to receive and accept an offer, stay at the job longer, and perform better. This all adds up to spending less time on the hiring process, reducing turnover, and increasing overall productivity."[11]

5. **Employee-Led Recruiting/Maintaining Active Contacts**—By turning our employees into scouts through incentives that strengthen our teams, they become invested in those new hires, while at the same time their efforts enhance our pools by adding known commodities.

In the army it is referred to as recruiter duty, and most noncommissioned officers cycle through this type of leadership at some point in their career. The Department of the Army-selected recruiters are NCOs whose branches have nominated them for duty as recruiters. Each MOS (Military Occupational Skill) branch is responsible for assigning soldiers to special duties such as Recruiter. Drill Sergeants are selected in a similar fashion as they both involve additional training prior to being turned loose in pursuit of that mission. The same level of training, care, and commitment needs to accompany any employee referral program to achieve real and lasting success.

College fraternities do this with invitations to parties and events. No one sells the organization and its benefits better than the people that work there, those who experience the "real experience" versus those who are paid to sell the company. When your line item workers tell friends and colleagues why your company is such an awesome place to work, they are recruiting whether active or not. When you make a concerted effort to put into action such a plan by providing incentives such as hiring bonuses and other rewards, it proves more effective.

Maintaining active contacts aids in our ability to recruit directly or through shared contacts. The larger your network, the broader your contacts and higher the possibility of strengthening pools by supplying those pools with individuals who have the demonstrated skills that are a match for our openings.

6. **Brand Utilization and Professional Associations** work to generate a "buzz" or create interest in who you are as an organization and make people want to be part of that organization.

Colleges and universities do this all the time as they create energy, awareness, and desire to be a part of their success, their history, their legend. Branding is what cements that awareness and keeps their name, reputation, and desire *front of mind* when parents and prospective students are college shopping. In a Forbes article entitled "College Branding the Tipping Point" (2013),[12] Dooley reports that there are nearly 4,000 colleges and universities in the United States, and while they seem to be able to fill their seats, competition and elimination loom in the years to come as the "key differences in who survives won't be the academic output of the faculty or the amenities available to students. It will be a factor seemingly unrelated to the schools' mission: branding."[13]

Make no mistake, each college/university represents a *team*, and they are in competition for students, faculty, donors, corporate partnerships, media attention, naming rights, and a host of other considerations that strengthen their brand.

It starts with the name and goes into the creation of signage, color schemes, mascots, emblems, clothing, logos and iconic buildings, dorms, campus design, and layout working together to burn the brand into society as part of an elite experience. That experience extends an offer to join the *team*, not just any team but their team—providing you are the right fit for them, which is determined by a host of criteria in the selection process. Point being, they are "selective" in who they want on their team to represent them over the next four academic years and years to come as a successful alumnus.

As companies and organizations struggle to compete for top talent in today's global market, branding is a critical element of any successful plan to not only survive but thrive. It plays a vital role in attracting that talent by bringing them into the fold, giving them connection to the organization in a way that celebrates *team* throughout their stay.

In Summit, New Jersey, you're a Hilltopper and the *flame* that burns bright in the hearts and minds of the residents, business owners, and those fortunate to work there is found in the City's seal, the Board of Education's website, and community partners that share a pride in being part of the community. During the American Revolutionary War, Summit was known as "Beacon Hill," because bonfire beacons were lit on an eastern ridge in Summit to warn the New Jersey militiamen of approaching British troops.

According to Bloomberg, Summit ranked as the seventeenth highest-income place in America in 2017, seventy-second in 2018 (with an average household income of $220,971), and sixty-fifth in 2019. Part of that success is due to branding by pulling together all the greatness of the City's offerings combined with its distinguished history in one easily recognized symbol—the flame. That flame and the name Summit represent success and part of the American dream that all aspire to be part of, as evidenced in the 2020 Best Places according to Niche as #9 out of 413 Suburbs with the Best Public Schools in New Jersey, #11 out of 571 Places with the Best Public Schools in New Jersey and #12 Best Suburbs to Live in New Jersey.

Just as branding attracts potential home buyers to Summit, it serves to attract top talent to job offerings within the community. This example extends to any community, business, or organization interested in growth and vitality for continued longevity.

While branding attracts talent, professional associations allow us to distribute the brand through publication, speaking, holding positions of leadership, and pressing the flesh, which now, thanks to the Coronavirus, may become the air high five or disconnected fist pump.

Professional associations allow leaders, key personnel, and frontline supervisors to represent their organizations in ways that attract positive interest in those organizations from outsiders.

Think about any conference you have attended in which you sat through a workshop or presentation only to wish the presenter worked for you or your organization. At the end of any engaging presentation, those speakers are met by interested attendees that pepper them with questions to gain better insight into best practices and successful endeavors that can be transferred to their own organizations and careers in the pursuit of similar success. It allows us to mirror that success by grabbing hold of the accomplishments, ideas, and parts of their brand that can be transformed to strengthen our brand, improve our outcomes, and expand our networks.

That is how I landed Dennis Budinch, chief culture officer at Investors Bank, to write the forward for *Planning for Success: Strategies That Enhance the Process of Goal Attainment.* After hearing Dennis speak at a recent New Jersey School Boards Association Workshop in Atlantic City, NJ, I was taken by his charismatic approach to leadership and goals and knew we shared a common vision of leadership. The fact that Dennis represented Investors Bank with a strong brand appeal sealed the deal after a lengthy conversation on "Grit."

7. **Campus Recruiting and Retire Recruiting**—While campus recruiting focuses on those new to the workforce in an effort to attract new talent

and emerging leaders, retirees represent experienced talent that strengthens our pools, especially for short-term or part-time work.

College recruits provide employers a real advantage in acquiring new talent at a discount—based on limited experience, however, at the same time gaining fresh ideas accompanied by strong analytical, technical, and critical thinking/problem-solving skills. In education this talent pool is strongly dependent upon for not only full-time positions but staffing reserves in the form of long-term substitutes, leave replacements, and teacher aides that maintain stronger pools as they continue to gain experience and compete for full-time positions as they come available.

Ways to increase this effort are often tied to internship programs because they work for both parties (win-win), providing experience and opportunities for graduates and creation of staffing pools for businesses. Like anything worthwhile, in order for them to be productive, they need to be properly managed and overseen with a strong commitment to the candidate's success. Far too often, internship programs fail in companies that fail to provide proven success for its candidates, as word of mouth and unsupported progress kills off interest from future candidates.

Although retirees are not necessarily a long-term solution to staffing, they pose another added benefit in the hiring process—they come at a discount— often accepting lower wages as the additional income represents supplemental income to their pension and/or social security income. Add to this that most retirees are not looking for health benefits, and the cost of hiring goes down further.

With retirees, the strongest factor in strengthening the pool lies with the experience that they have accumulated over a lifetime of listening, observing, working, decision-making, and problem-solving. Those combined experiences represent a strong argument for considering this pool of labor in your applicant pools moving forward if you have not already done so. The task and challenge remain to properly vet these candidates to ensure they still have value for your organization, and that is achieved through the interview process—"square two."

Chapter 3

Selecting Talent

Staffing organizations begin by selecting the right *talent* to bolster the *team(s)* within those organizations and that means ensuring your interview process is *rigorous*, *organized*, and *real*. Soft interviews often lead to poor choices as candidates are not properly screened, challenged, or vetted to determine the best choice and more importantly the appropriate choice.

Interviewing is how we comb through the talent to find *who is right* for us *right now* (where we are) and for the *future* (where we are going). We are looking to attain those who not only bring value (knowledge and skill) but share our vision to join the effort in accomplishing our mission. That requires energy, determination, and drive—all attributes we need to uncover in our interviews.

The interview process is the most critical step in the hiring process. It serves as our opportunity to vet candidates as part of our responsibility to find those with the *right stuff* to bring continued success to our organizations. The challenge is in selecting the right candidate and more importantly maintaining that feeling of success in hiring over time. The best evidence of this is when we see individuals who not only achieve but excel—and that is the *difference maker* when differentiating good from great.

One of the best examples of this is the quote from legendary 1980 Gold Medal Ice Hockey Coach Herb Brooks when selecting his team against the pushback of sponsors and his assistant coach Craig Patrick, "I'm not looking for the best players; I'm looking for the right ones." That's a powerful quote that teaches us to work for a greater achievement than any one individual; it is the essence of strength through combined talent that is only possible in teams.

Good employees come to work every day, and they perform necessary tasks, functions, and responsibilities that help keep us moving in achieving our mission; whereas great employees do the same thing but at a faster rate, and they have the value add of exceeding the standard in all aspects of performance: Quality and Quantity of Work, Knowledge of Job, Work Habits, Cooperation and Human Relations, Dependability, and Initiative (figure 3.1).

Those who exceed these basic standards are great hires, and they become great employees and great leaders regardless of where they are in the hierarchy. They are the right hires for jobs we need to achieve our goals. They are the difference makers and they are human resources.

From time to time I have found myself defending a *position* over a *person* by simply acknowledging the need for the position—just not necessarily that person. Simply put it recognizes that the individual is not right for the job and perhaps they never were. That questions the hiring process and allows us to review, analyze, and adjust our hiring practices to improve our outcomes

Figure 3.1   **Basic Performance Standards.** *Source*: Self-created.

going forward. In some cases, those individuals are inherited; however, they are with us and were probably hired by someone in the past.

When hiring works as it should, we are left with positive endorsements from a leader who looks over their staff and calls out an individual by stating, "One of the best hires I ever made." Notice the context of "one"—this stipulates there have been more and there should be plenty if the organization is committed to proper interviews and the leader puts in the time, energy, and focus to ensure committees are properly staffed, prepped, and equipped for all interviews.

Dedicated leaders often remark about great hires and not-so-great hires they have contributed to over their careers—they do not waste time talking about good hires. These are leaders who own their mistakes in addition to celebrating their successes; these are leaders with a true love for the company or organization they helped build, and they recognize a deep connection, pride, and responsibility for its continued success. The opposite finds poor leaders who refer to good versus bad hiring decisions they have made as if it comes down to luck or simply the luck of the draw (the pool). Truth be told we all own a few bad hires, and it serves as a cause for pause to reflect why it happened and more importantly how can we avoid such mistakes in the future.

So how do we improve the outcome? How do we increase the odds of landing the right talent for our organization? It begins with better preparation in the interview process to make it more effective and improve those odds to produce more great hires. Let's take a look at how we can improve our interviews.

After we have obtained the necessary talent from our pools, we must be careful to perform a proper and thorough interview that ensures against allowing weak, unprepared, or incompetent individuals to join our ranks. "Caveat emptor"—Latin for "Let the buyer beware"—has a familiar ring in hiring as we do not wish to regret our hiring decisions, and trust me, we are buying something here as the exchange for services is founded in salary and benefits that are driven by the expectations and perceived value of the individual.

So preparing for our interviews should be a respected process that ensures we are as ready for the interview as the candidate who has spent a considerable amount of time prepping to provide answers that impress, intrigue, and often seduce interviewers into grabbing onto what they perceive is a "hot commodity" or an individual in "high demand." But are they the right person for the job and more importantly the right fit for your organization? That's why this process step here is so important. A bad hire has the possibility of costing organizations in unemployment claims, law suits, loss of productivity, loss of good workers, and bad morale.

Too often I have seen individuals who interviewed great; however, their actual work failed to measure up. Likewise, I have seen individuals who were stellar performers who developed into great leaders, but they were not good interviewers.

Two of the best hires I have ever made were both internal candidates and both moved up into director positions. One nailed the interview which had been more of a Pro-forma exercise since he had been in the role of acting for months. It allowed him to demonstrate his skill set and provided an opportunity to lead and manage the department.

The other guy was nervous. He had never been in a leadership role before, and it showed as the interview quickly turned into one of the worst interviews I have ever conducted. He walked in as a favorite and walked out as a distant consideration, having fallen victim to nerves and lack of experience. Despite his performance in the interview, I saw promise, commitment, and potential that needed a chance to show. Following the interview, I gave him immediate and honest feedback, decided to give him another chance, and began coaching him for the next round. He had the knowledge and skill set for the position and a true mastery of the work to be supervised as he had done it for years.

What was missing, besides confidence, was the 30,000-foot view in his answers during the first interview. I handed him a magazine article on vision, mission, and directing teams and told him to read it and apply it to how he envisioned the team under his leadership. "Tell us where you want to go and how you intend on getting the team there," I told him.

He showed up at the next interview days later and owned it! Not only were the nerves gone, but he was also focused and ready to answer each question in a way that permeated a level of understanding reserved for seasoned managers. He put forth a vision that pointed to the kind of future we needed. The second he walked out of the room, my boss turned and said, "We found our candidate!"

He was offered the position and it worked. A decade later he is still with the organization and delivering one success after another.

Our job here is to tell the difference between good hires and bad, by rooting out those who are masters of disguise as we go through the volley of questions and more importantly apply tasks/tests to prove competencies that are real and possessed by the candidate. Otherwise, we can be routed by pretenders who are skilled in deception as they can easily manipulate interviewers who find themselves unprepared or out of their depth when interviewing. This requires planning, strategy, and training to develop and implement techniques aimed at acquiring successful candidates from the *"talent group"* selected for the next step in the hiring process—the interview.

For decades the need for proper preparation has been recognized as the single most important aspect of achieving successful interviews. In a 2014 Harvard Business Review article entitled "Strategies of Effective Interviewing" that concept was restated from the words of Samuel G. Trull, an engineer and college professor who had written on the subject in 1964 over half a century before, "The lack of adequate planning for an interview is the greatest single fault found in my studies of the interviewing process. All too often, the inexperienced interviewer launches into a discussion only to find midway through that his preparation is incomplete. A moderate amount of preplanning can easily obviate such unfortunate occurrences."[1]

Like any task before us, the more planning that goes into preparation of that task, the better the outcome—and interviewing is no exception. Just as candidates who prep for the interview experience success by being prepared, ready, and able to take on anticipated questions, you need to be ready to ascertain the degree of their skill set, depth of their knowledge, and their ability to think on the fly. If you're not ready, they will not be able to demonstrate their degree of skill or depth of knowledge in the interview. As such you place them at a clear disadvantage by bringing all candidates up to an easy line where no one emerges from the pack regarding skill, knowledge, and creativity. Instead of an effective interview designed to secure a great candidate, it becomes simply a failed opportunity.

To prevent failed opportunities due to poor preparation, HR directors should ensure all interviews within the organization are being conducted based on the following techniques.

TEN EFFECTIVE INTERVIEW TECHNIQUES

1. **Selection of Committee Members**—Put the right people on the committee, select individuals for the interview committee that have knowledge

of the position, responsibilities and interactions with that position. When you talk team, the importance of having team members in the interviews to determine others who will become part of that team is not only important, it is critical to get their insights, feelings, and sense of compatibility. Too often supervisors or managers interview in a vacuum and forget the need to include members from the team.

Case in Point—when hiring one of my assistants (junior administrator) the candidate who was selected later remarked to my secretary how impressed she was with the fact that she (my secretary) was on the interview team and there past normal office hours. That not only spoke well of our team and their commitment, it set the tone for expectations.

2. **Use a Greeter and a Facilitator**—This brings direction and order to the process and provides the candidates with an impression of professionalism and sense of importance for the position. The greeter and the facilitator should not be the same person. This keeps both parties more on their toes and guards against appearing too casual when at this point in the process you want to appear more formal.

3. **Provide an Appropriate Setting**—The importance and tone of an interview begin with the setting and impression it gives off. Is it one that gives off a sense of order, care, and importance? Or does it come off as hurried, neglectful, and sloppy? Just as candidates are looking to make and leave a good impression on organizations considering their employment, those organizations should consider the impression they are giving off on the potential new hires who may be considering whether they want to accept an offer.

   Determining a suitable location for the interviews should include the following objectives:
   a. Privacy to avoid unnecessary interruptions and maintain focus on the interview.
   b. Avoid distractions to include heavy foot traffic, windows to busy office happenings, or noise that could break concentration for the candidate or members of the committee.
   c. Avoid the "fish bowl" room where others can observe the interview; this immediately places the candidate in a state of self-consciousness and takes away from the focus of the interview.

4. **Review of Candidate's Documents**—Ensure packets containing each candidate's resume and cover letter are sent to all committee members

prior to the interview for review and preparation. Be sure to have these on hand during the interview to refresh their notes and revisit any sections that warrant further explanation or exploration. Remember these documents are typically crafted from templates to look impressive and read well; however, it is often what is not included that should raise concern and generate questions.

To make the point I refer back to an interview I once conducted with a facilities supervisor for a custodial position.

We had spent the afternoon interviewing candidates from our pool of qualified applicants that had already been interviewed with the building principal (first round), and we were just not finding the right candidate, or at least someone we were really excited about.

We were ready for the last candidate when my secretary (the greeter) brought in a gentleman that appeared to be a serious upgrade from what we had been looking at, starting with his appearance: shoes shined, pressed shirt and pants, clean shaven with the general look of someone who takes pride in their appearance. He was articulate, detailed in his responses, and appeared knowledgeable with general cleaning and maintenance tasks.

As the supervisor continued to ask questions, I had already mentally moved him to my selection and at this point was waiting to follow up with salary and benefit information in order to move his candidacy forward and begin reference checks.

It was at this point that it jumped right out at me, as I perused his resume—a ten-year gap in employment—how had I missed such a gap? It was now glaring at me like the Grand Canyon as I looked up and interrupted the conversation to question, "Excuse me," I said, "I notice you skipped ten years in your employment history, can you explain where you were during that time and what you were doing?" He didn't flinch and stated, "I was around." I looked incredulous and pushed him further, "What do you mean around?" I said in a stern concerned voice, "Doing what," I said, "Give me one job you had during this time?"

As he responded, his entire demeanor began to change rapidly, and his voice took on an air of aggravation and contempt as he stated, "I don't know . . . I had a lot of jobs."

"Not good enough," I said, "you have to be able to account for such a gap!" At this point, I knew the interview was over but pressed for an answer mostly because I could not believe this was happening, and in all my years of interviewing, I had never come across something so bizarre. "Were you on a ship, were you in lock up?" I questioned, then followed with, "You know we drug test."

His response was nothing short of amazing as the color drained from his face and his voice changed to one of alarm as he asked, "What, right now?"

We were done—as he stormed out the door with his resume he had grabbed out of the supervisor's hand.

The takeaway—don't just look at it, read it!

5. **Formulate Relevant Questions**—By ensuring members of the interview committee review the job description prior to the interview, they will be better prepared to ask relevant questions that directly relate to the performance requirements and responsibilities of the position. This is a simple yet often overlooked point.

6. **Develop Structured Interview Questions**—Prepare a standard set of questions in advance for all candidates to answer—this strengthens the process by ensuring the integrity of the process (all being equal) and allows the committee to compare answers to the same questions. Once the set questions are asked, additional questions or follow-up questions can be asked if needed and time permits. Not only does a structured interview help keep the process on track; it keeps the process from running afoul of any legal restrictions.

Structured interview questions are job-related. They're friendlier to equal opportunity since all candidates face the same questions in the same order. Structured interviews allow for greater objectivity. They work well in team hiring environments and group interviews where individual biases are less likely to interfere. They also make it simpler to provide interview feedback to candidates you're keeping in your talent pool.[2]

7. **Master Time Management**—Establish an appropriate amount of time for each interview by giving each candidate the necessary time to answer questions in a thorough manner. Don't rush it, be respectful of their time and that of your committee members. Remember, these individuals are often taking personal time off from their current job in order to meet your schedule in hopes of gaining a better opportunity. While some look forward to it, others anxiously await it, but in either case, they typically

spend extra time getting ready, selecting their clothes, leaving extra time to arrive early and travel to places unfamiliar, leaving questions of where to park, what door to go in, and do they have a last opportunity to check their look before being called in.

So what is an appropriate amount of time? Conventional wisdom says forty-five minutes to an hour is customary for interviews. This leaves time for committee discussion of first impressions and key takeaways once the candidate is ushered out before the next one is brought in. This will prove helpful in the final analysis as it becomes a solid measure in justifying the final recommendation, thus validating the process as thorough, detailed, and defensible to outside criticism—this is especially true of high-profile positions or political ones.

8. **Schedule Multiple Rounds**—One interview alone is not enough to ascertain the true character of a person. Having a minimum of two separate interviews allows the committee to see consistencies and inconsistencies any candidate may have. It also provides an opportunity for candidates to start with their reflections of the previous interview: Did they leave anything out; do they wish to expand on any answer previously given? This is also a great opportunity to dig deeper into any area of concern that the committee may have or allow greater clarity in answers previously given. It is surprising how ranking can change after the second round of interviews, and yet, it also provides more solid thinking in the group's selection when your #1 candidate continues to stay above the pack, this is actually what we hope for, but now it's what we know.

9. **Debrief**—Debriefing between rounds gives committee members and the chairperson an opportunity to compare notes and exchange thoughts, impressions, and knowledge as they attempt to build consensus and rank candidates as the process evolves. Once the last candidate has completed their interview, the group needs to move to the final analysis to compare, contrast, and rank individuals to determine top candidates in ascertaining the right fit for the position.

The perspectives of others are why they are on the committee in the first place and often lead to a complete picture of the candidate(s) and their performance(s) throughout the process.

In order to benefit from the participation of committee members, they need to be heard and considered. If not, the committee is just a sham, and the process itself can be called into question. Worse yet is the damage it does to the team and future requests or appointments for participation in future hiring. Would you want to be on that committee?

This is a critical step and one that needs to be valued by all members of the committee including the manager who has the final say—he/she must remain cognizant of the fact that if no one else on the team supports their choice in the selection process, that individual will be hard pressed to find support from the team once they come on board. Even if they get it at some point in the future, it will definitely be a rough start and a considerable delay before they are able to reach acceptance; however, the odds are not in their favor and the truth is they may not ever be fully accepted.

The takeaway: Process, Process, Process—develop a process, adhere to the process, adjust the process as necessary based on feedback, results, or deficiencies and let the process work by producing the right choice. If you do not feel confident in the final selection of the candidate, start over. Never settle for the wrong person just to fill the position. When this happens, leaders within organizations knowingly or unknowingly weaken the team. Often, they justify the move with lines such as "they were the best of the bunch" and "the field is pretty slim," or the weakest of all settlement quotes, "There's really nobody else out there!"

Taking a lesser qualified candidate is one thing because you can always train them; however, taking someone with a bad attitude or less than desirable attributes means you are settling for less than the best and exposing the rest of the team to a negative disrupter. Such action is short sited and detrimental to the success of the group, given enough bad choices and you weaken the team on a larger scale that will harm the effort, drag down production, erode efficiency, and compromise the effectiveness of the team; left uncorrected such action could jeopardize the future of the organization.

If we begin to experience *"slim pickings"* in our interview selections, it's time to move on to a *different* or *new* field. Expand the net, enlarge the pool, or rethink your screening process for the selection of interviewees. A great tip that has become more dependent of late, due to the global shutdowns with the Coronavirus, is virtual interviews which allow for quick access to view and evaluate candidates prior to actual committee interviewing. In this step, one or two individuals can screen a larger group of potential interviewees by conducting ten- to fifteen-minute conversations designed to find good candidates worth bringing to the committee or department manager.

Screening interview questions include basics that help ensure we are looking at the right candidates and ensure we are not wasting the time of committee members who are being pulled off other efforts in order to assist with the staffing function. In order to accomplish this task, Human Resource officers typically pose questions designed to ensure candidates are qualified and worth pursuing. Indeed, a worldwide employment-related search engine recently shared this list of sample questions for job seekers to consider:[3]

- *What are you looking for in a position?*
- *Tell me about yourself.*
- *What reasons do you have for leaving your most recent job?*
- *Describe your current job responsibilities?*
- *What drew you to this position?*
- *What compensation are you looking for?*
- *What management style suits you best?*
- *When could you start working if you were selected for this role?*
- *What has been your biggest achievement so far?*
- *What are your strengths? What are your weaknesses?*
- *Where do you see yourself in five years?*
- *How do you cope with stress?*
- *What motivates you in a job?*
- *Why should we hire you?*
- *Do you have any specific questions about this role?*

10. **Communicate Next Steps**—Don't leave them hanging; the worst feeling for a candidate after an interview is not knowing what's next and what your intentions are moving forward. The best way to keep quality candidates engaged and committed to your process is keeping them actively informed on their progress and that should start immediately following the last question.

The best way to avoid an uncomfortable situation or awkward pauses is to have a skilled facilitator regain control of the flow by either asking the candidate if they have any questions at this point or simply informing them of the group's intentions and time expectations for making a decision. Failure to do so can run the risk of losing a great prospect that might have assumed you were not interested in them and simply moved on and found other opportunities. Keep in mind if they are not moving forward or being selected, they deserve to be informed as soon as possible. While some companies or organizations simply send a letter, a phone call is more personal, appreciated, and respected especially among high-level candidates who you may run into at future events such as conferences, workshops, and professional trainings.

By applying these ten interview techniques, you can ensure you not only have a process but have a process that works—one that is valued by the members of the organization who participate in the process and those who count on the process to yield great hires for the team. In order for that process to be successful, it needs to be open and honest. An open and honest process generates the best candidates with the greatest possibilities of moving teams forward in reaching their goals quicker. When managers start bypassing or ignoring the process with preselection of individuals who may not be the best available, they comprise not only the process but the team.

Part II

THE TOUGHER SIDE OF HR

Chapter 4

Thinning the Herd

Talk to any HR director and they will tell you firing people is the last thing they want to do—as a matter of course it is really the final option for a number of factors starting with the investment in both time and money. Organizations in the United States spend about $77 billion on average for training each year according to the 2019 Training Industry Report released by Training magazine.[1] That training is seen as an investment in the company's largest investment—human capital. Once hired, candidates become assets and smart companies set out to ensure they keep those assets as long as possible while maximizing their investment to ensure maximum production and greater success.

Although turnover is a natural event in any business or industry and efforts are constantly underway to develop new talent and increase our talent pools, the cost of replacement due to termination becomes an unbudgeted expense and depending on the amount of training and development spent on the particular employee—even costlier. Therefore, we should try to exhaust reasonable attempts to address, mitigate, and correct poor performance and unacceptable behaviors prior to considering termination.

"Recruitment is expensive and may not yield a candidate with the skills of your poorly performing worker. When you hired the professional in question, there were reasons why you thought they were suited to the job role and these are unlikely to have completely dissolved. What's more likely is that the employee has become disillusioned with the company or is annoyed at something else. Find out what this is and do your best to resolve it. This way you save on the

time, hassle and expense of recruitment, while also getting the best out of an
employee that is already familiar with your brand and ethos."[2]

Basically, you can't fire everybody and a team without veterans is a team without leaders! Yet, the reality is some individuals do not improve regardless of the additional time, effort, and resources afforded to them. Likewise, some veterans exhibit a concerning behavior referred to in the military as "R.O.A.D"—Retired On Active Duty—therefore providing little to no benefit as they command higher wages and benefits without the sharing of knowledge, skill, and mentoring for less-experienced workers. You know the type; they show up enough to be present and conserve energy as they seemingly stay engaged. Regardless of where individuals fall on the years of service continuum, we must consider the cost of maintaining a disruptive influence on the team and company as a whole.

- "The U.S. Department of Labor says the cost of a bad hire can reach up to 30 percent of the employee's first-year earnings."[3]
- "The Undercover Recruiter reports bad hires can cost $240,000 in expenses. Those are broken down into costs related to hiring, pay and retention."[4]
- "CareerBuilder says 74 percent of companies who made a poor hire lost an average of $14,900 per poor hire."[5]

Nothing is tougher than having to take negative actions against individuals such as separation, termination, and firing, even though these actions produce positive results for the organization. While unpleasant and disruptive in the short-term, it is often necessary for long-term improvement of teams and, in some cases, the only way to save the organization itself. Anyone in a management role can tell you—*it happens, it's not fun*—but it must be done.

Like any decision of consequence, it should not be done in haste or in a vacuum but only after careful consideration of behavior, action, or circumstance. In some cases, this may require placing the individual on leave (with or without pay) pending investigation into the matter to allow ample opportunity to gather the appropriate facts prior to issuing a final decision. Yet, other times depending on the severity of the injury or potential harm that exists endangering employees or the organization, termination can take place immediately. "Actions that jeopardize the organization itself or the reputation of the organization are reasons for immediate termination of an employee. This includes all forms of theft, whether the theft is against the company, such as property, or the theft is against another employee, such as stealing a coworker's wallet. Many companies will also terminate an employee for committing criminal acts outside of the workplace."[6] Actions that place other employees in danger are also seen as a cause for immediate termination. "This includes violence, vandalism and knowingly endangering other employees by bringing dangerous items, such as weapons, to work."[7]

So *how* and *when* as managers should we act and to *what* degree are we held accountable for those actions? Let's start with the accountability piece. The short answer involving accountability, the *"what,"* is 100 percent—it's part of the job! It reminds me of a sign I recently came across in Bottle King of all places that read, *"Yes, Doing Your Job is Part of Your Job."*

The longer answer as to the *how* and *when* we should act as managers to take such action is swiftly (*how*), regardless of the time it takes to make the final decision (*when*) which can range from immediate—involving a clear threat to persons, property, or the organization—to timely based on a thorough investigation of claims, charges, or actions that are inconsistent with the organization's code of ethics, standards, or acceptable behaviors. Keep in mind, these are fireable offenses or they can be settled with disciplinary action if appropriate. Much different than performance-based dismissals which are tied to performance and memorialized in memos, observations, and evaluations.

The connective tissue to good practices regarding tough actions such as termination of employment is *training* and *reliance* on strong HR practices coupled with the guidance of a knowledgeable labor attorney. Law firms who specialize in labor law provide quick and effective advice when needed to expedite the difficult decisions that need to happen in real time. Human resource officers are skilled in dealing with these difficult personnel decisions and typically know when to consult attorneys. While attorneys offer specific guidance and advice to avoid legal ramifications and guard against exposure, policy is in place to insulate and protect the organization from violations of individual rights related to labor law.

As such, managers need to review employment policies and stay up to date on changes with respect to labor relations and labor law. This is accomplished by reading bulletins, newsletters and attending workshops, seminars, and conferences. Additionally, try pulling out (hard copy) or pulling up (electronic) the actual policy manual from time to time and especially during consideration of any violations related to conduct. Supporting your actions and activities with an approved policy is a safe way to guard against liability and exposure—that is why it exists.

We have all heard the sayings, "Shape up or ship out"—"Straighten Up and Fly Right." These phrases are both throwbacks to the 1940s, a time when the armed forces dominated our culture with respect to attitude, service, and expectations of conduct.

In companies it was a basic ultimatum to someone to improve their performance or behavior or risk being canned. In the military, at that time, the threat meant being sent overseas to a combat zone.

"Straighten Up and Fly Right" might seem to have belonged to the Air Force but was actually derived from a story that Nat King Cole often heard his father, a pastor, use to deliver a message of improving one's behavior or attitude to perform better. He put it to music in the winter of 1943 and that message was amplified, reaching a larger audience as the tune became a number one hit on the Harlem Hit Parade for ten nonconsecutive weeks and peaked at number nine on the pop charts.[8]

So basically at the time of the sayings, the 1940s, it was understood that individuals needed to get their act together or they would get the boot. Today most companies consider the *right to terminate without cause* as part of the rights covered under the legal distinction of *at-will employment*. While each state in the United States, with the exception of Montana, is considered an at-will employment state, employers must comply with both federal law and applicable state laws (figure 4.1).

All fifty states in the United States and Washington, DC, are at-will employment states; however, some states have exemptions such as Public, Implied, and Good Faith Covenants. As represented in figure 4.1, we see both the Pacific and Rocky Mountain Region with the largest exemptions, each with two states having all three exemptions (Alaska, California, Idaho, and Utah); and the North East and South East with four states (Rhode Island, Florida, Georgia, and Louisiana) with no exemptions.

"At-will means an employer can terminate an employee at any time for any reason, except an illegal one, or for no reason without incurring legal liability."[9] As such, a critical resource for any organization remains a highly qualified labor attorney. Additionally, this represents a critical area of professional

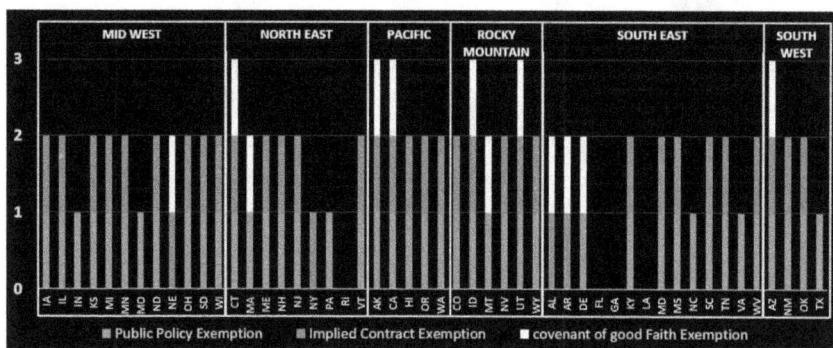

Figure 4.1 States by Region with Exemptions to At-Will Employment. *Source*: Data compiled from worldpopulationreview.com; self-created.

development for needed training of supervisors and managers to avoid running afoul of the labor laws leading to poor decisions that bring costly penalties.

In today's PC culture fraught with litigation and increased scrutiny over individual rights, not only do we need to ensure we have a valid case to support any decision to terminate we need to document our steps and adhere to established policies consistent with discipline, notice, and procedures. Such policies need to be reviewed by a labor attorney to ensure consistency with all state and federal labor laws. Failure to adopt and follow such protocol puts management and the company or organization at risk, as the action becomes challengeable and difficult to defend.

Such exposure will more often than not bring about negative consequences of a wrongful termination suit, which may involve violation of federal antidiscrimination laws or a contractual breach. "A wrongful termination claim can be filed in a court of law if an employee believes he or she has been 'illegally' fired from the job. Such claims result from an alleged violation of federal or state anti-discrimination laws, employment contracts or labor laws, including whistle-blower laws."[10] Specific violations include sexual harassment, constructive dismissal, discrimination, breach of contract, whistleblowing, retaliation, protected time off, and policy violations.

So not only have we concluded that as managers *firing* is part of the job, and although unpleasant, it is a necessary part of improving team performance. So how do we improve our process and manage the task without creating bigger problems for ourselves, our teams, and our organizations?

We start by being honest, deliberate, and transparent. Individuals who are let go (terminated) should never be walked out in a daze of confusion as to why. If we as managers have done our job, termination should not be a surprise but, instead, a follow-through of what has already been conveyed as the ultimate consequence to poor performance, consistent violations of policy and procedures, inappropriate behaviors, or a necessary result of a major violation. The later, a major violation is easy to comprehend and easy to follow—it just happened and it is extremely serious—resulting in immediate termination.

Poor performance, on the other hand, requires written evidence or documentation in the form of write-ups, observations, evaluations, and corrective action plans that note specific deficiencies or violations with increasing disciplinary measures tied to material consequences.

In 2000 an attorney working with an established NJ law firm, Lindabury, McCormick, Estabrook, and Cooper, introduced a group of young administrators to the concept of progressive discipline and how it generates evidence needed to support the actions building up to termination of an employee. I was among that group.

Fifteen years later, he would establish his own firm, SCIARRILLO COR-NELL, MERLINO, MCKEEVER & OSBORNE, LLC, specializing in Education Law with a concentration on employment, labor relations/negotiation, and policy in addition to three other areas.

Notice the connection of employment to labor relations, negotiations, and policy as they all intersect and provide an excellent case for Venn diagrams. Years earlier, the military had already ingrained in me the concept of routine evaluations in the form of quarterlies, semiannuals, and annual evaluations, stressing the need to ensure behaviors both good and bad are documented to mitigate and improve poor performance as well as reward good performance. Together these concepts—*progressive discipline* and *timely evaluations*—provide an ironclad strategy to mitigate, moderate, and, if necessary, terminate.

In court cases, evidence is broken down into four basic types: demonstrative, real, testimonial, and documentary. Documentary evidence is most often considered real evidence. It is any type of evidence that helps to document the issue being discussed in the trial; in the case of a wrongful termination, it would be the documents laid out in the above paragraph—write-ups, observations, evaluations, and corrective action plans—that serve as confirmation to the actions we have taken, thus making them defensible.

Remember, our goal is not to terminate but to get employees back on track and responsive to what is acceptable and what is expected. Termination is our last option, and as such progressive discipline works to change those behaviors and give employees ample opportunity to take corrective action in avoidance of being terminated.

However, once we have reached the point of no return, progressive discipline is what backs up our action at the moment (the firing) and supports our actions leading up to that moment (the paper trail). Therefore, progressive discipline serves as a productive tool to correct bad behavior and hopefully avoid letting people go.

Progressive discipline comes down to three basic things:

1. You need to be specific
2. You need to be consistent and
3. You need to write it down

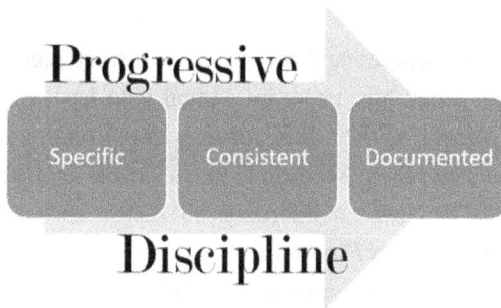

Figure 4.2 **Progressive Discipline.** *Source*: Self-created.

It is a structured process containing graduated disciplinary steps including verbal and written warnings, suspension, withholding of increments and ultimately termination of employment. It is designed to improve employee performance, correct a problem or pattern of negative behavior(s), and provide coaching, but it also serves to document the effort. Done right, progressive discipline can provide structure or order in an organization, set standards for managers and supervisors, and provide protection against employment claims related to wrongful termination.

Nolo, the web's largest libraries of consumer-friendly legal information reports, captures the benefits of progressive discipline in an article written by Lisa Guerin, author of *The Manager's Legal Handbook*, *Dealing with Problem Employees*, and *Workplace Investigations*.

THE BENEFITS OF PROGRESSIVE DISCIPLINE[11]

- Allow managers to intervene and correct employee behavior at the first sign of trouble
- Enhance communication between managers and employees
- Help managers achieve higher performance and productivity from their employees
- Improve employee morale and retention by demonstrating that there are rewards for good performance and consequences for poor performance
- Avoid expensive replacement costs
- Ensure consistency and fairness in dealing with employee problems and
- Lay the groundwork for fair, legally defensible employment termination for employees who cannot or will not improve.

So when the time comes and we have no further recourse other than to part ways with a bad hire or an individual who has exhausted all remedies for improvement, is there a better way to *cut bait* or *pull the trigger* or *simply end the misery*? According to an article that appeared in the Harvard Business Review on February 2016, the answer is a resounding yes! *The Right Way to Fire Someone*,[12] according to Rebecca Knight, "Don't drag your feet." "The prospect of firing someone you've worked with for years—particularly someone you know well and respect—is daunting, but you mustn't let your personal agony delay the conversation."[13] Not only do I agree with the advice, but I also subscribe to the same school of thought and have counseled many managers, supervisors, and colleagues over the years to do what is right for the organization, which in turn benefits the team. To delay the inevitable only prolongs the agony and places the organization at greater risk. Not sure, check with your attorney—labor attorneys perk up when they hear words like *hostile work environment*, *harassment*, *retaliation*, and *discrimination* being used by employees as they signal potential lawsuits.

Instead, we must carry out the unpopular task before the lack of action results in lower morale, reduced productivity, poor service, and significant damage to trust. As leaders, we must work just as hard to retain trust as we did to earn it.

When we fail to act we fail to lead. When we fail to lead we lose the trust and respect of those on the team who are doing the right thing and expect us to make the tough decisions we get paid to make.

Keeping weak performers or allowing individuals to terrorize the rest of the team is not only poor management; it is a recipe for disaster, and the one walked out the door could be you.

How we act is key, and word choice can help—be honest, be direct, and be kind. You've already decided to let the individual go; you should make every effort to deliver that news in a positive way that underscores the needs of the organization while at the same time demonstrating compassion for the individual that needs to move on and go forward from the experience to hopefully learn from their mistakes or simply find a better fit. Offer to provide a reference, if possible, and ensure they leave with an understanding of hope for a better future. Sometimes things just don't work out. Remember these are not the individuals who are being terminated for stealing or criminal activity—so you want to avoid treating them as such.

While unpleasant and upsetting there are ways to accomplish the task and put it into less threating language such as separation rather than firing. Even in less favorable situations the tone makes the music, and a better choice of words can help de-escalate a tense situation.

Once while meeting with an employee and his union representative following an investigation into theft-of-time, it was clear the employee was going to be let go. After the employee was confronted with the overwhelming evidence, he looked up and asked, "Am I being fired?" "No," I responded, "Just separated from duty, I need your keys and your badge." I then let the HR director take him for formal out-processing. He knew he was being terminated; it wasn't necessary to use the term fired—even Disney softens the message by stating, "Find your happiness elsewhere!"

Chapter 5

The Purpose of Evaluations

Making the grade—JD Powers & Associates—Blue Ribbon Schools—5 Star Ratings—US News & World Report's Rankings—Best in Class, Best in Show—Grade A.

Today we evaluate everything—we evaluate buildings, programs, contractors, and doctors, we evaluate restaurants, stores, and online retail experiences, and we rank cars, hotels, airlines, and vacations. Constantly comparing, rating, and judging performance, experiences, and satisfaction against expectations, standards, and results. So is it any wonder that we compare individuals by measuring their productivity, gauging their abilities, and reflecting on their overall contributions as we evaluate our teams?

> There have been debates around employee evaluations and some say it's time to put an end to it. But, while big companies like Adobe have abolished the traditional rating-based performance reviews, 69% of companies still conduct annual or semi-annual employee evaluation in one form or another.[1]

Evaluations are at the heart of improvement—they allow us to determine value, analyze activities, understand how things work and determine merit, regardless of what it is we are evaluating.

Evaluation of staff is no exception; this tool allows us to measure job performance, capture patterns of behavior both positive and negative, as well as pointing out strengths and weaknesses. We are providing individuals with an instant update with respect to formative evaluations and more detailed reports encompassing longer periods of time in the case of summative evaluations such as semiannual and annual.

So what exactly is an evaluation when it comes to personnel, and why do we need them as managers? The answer begins with the description of evaluation: the act or result of evaluating a situation that requires careful evaluation: determination of the value, nature, character, or quality of something or someone.[2] As to why we need them—their purpose—the answer remains consistent with the theme of this book on team building—*strength*—as in strengthening our teams through evaluation of performance.

In business, when we evaluate program, we employ a systematic assessment of the program or part(s) of it to gauge and determine the viability of the program and its appropriateness as it relates to goals and expected outcomes. We assess its overall effectiveness in determination of whether to continue, modify, or eliminate the program. Likewise, we consider the resources allocated to the program and decide whether those resources are adequately apportioned or if they should be adjusted either up or down in furtherance of continued operations over other programs—in essence, ranking the importance of the program compared to other programs with competing resources. The same is true of personnel and specifically which personnel, who is worth the investment, and who, as we found in the last chapter, is not.

"Evaluation is not simply about assessing whether an initiative was a success or failure. Instead, evaluation is about creating the information and data about the initiative's success and why. Evaluation findings can lead to more effective and efficient program delivery."[3] Again the same is true of people; those worth investing in or continuing to invest in are those who produce success through effectiveness and efficiency the *value-add* we look for in great employees. These are the types of employees that strengthen teams. Evaluations help to improve performance of all employees, both those in need of improvement and those who are already high performers, as it keeps them sharp, engaged, and focused.

In education we rely on both the formative and summative evaluations to gauge success in what students gain during the instruction or lesson (formative) versus what they have learned by the end of a section or marking period (summative). It delivers a quick (low stakes) feedback with a formative evaluation, providing guidance for the student. In contrast, a summative evaluation provides a detailed (high stakes) measure or assessment of overall progress for the student.

This also helps us determine progress with respect to the teacher (our employee) as they are held to the standards developed by both State and Federal Departments of Education and the expectations of the district as we remain responsible to our stakeholders. "Formative evaluations are designed to encourage development and improvement within an ongoing activity (or person, product, program, etc.). Summative evaluation, in contrast, is used to assess whether the results of the object being evaluated (program, intervention, person, etc.) met the stated goals."[4]

These broad categories, formative and summative, carry over into other types of evaluations, including, but not limited to, employee performance. They help us to measure performance and provide feedback to those evaluated, to make improvements, or continue to act in ways that bring value to the department, section, and organization. Formative evaluations provide information that improves initiatives by examining those initiatives, their implementation, or delivery.

This is the case with instruction in a classroom or procedures developed to manage an aspect of the operation, for example, purchasing or accounting. Summative evaluations are more encompassing as they look at outcomes of a given initiative allowing individuals to gain insights based on specific points of data to make effective decisions and assist with judgments related to the overall merit of the initiative based on a set of criteria.

Understanding the difference between formative and summative evaluations allows us to utilize them properly in order to strengthen our process of evaluations and strengthen our teams by strengthening our members. Observations are a great tool to motivate and inspire those eager to perform well and those looking for immediate feedback and reassurance that they are measuring up by meeting or, better yet, exceeding the standards (expectations). To make them more effective, start by communicating the expectations (performance standards) and the evaluation process, so everyone has a clear understanding of what is expected (performance) and what to expect (evaluations) in order to succeed.

STEP 1 — Establish Performance Standards

STEP 2 — Develop Evaluation Form

STEP 3 — Define Performance Measurement

STEP 4 — Communicate Performance Expectations

STEP 5 — Schedule Face-To-Face Meetings

STEP 6 — Set Target Goals

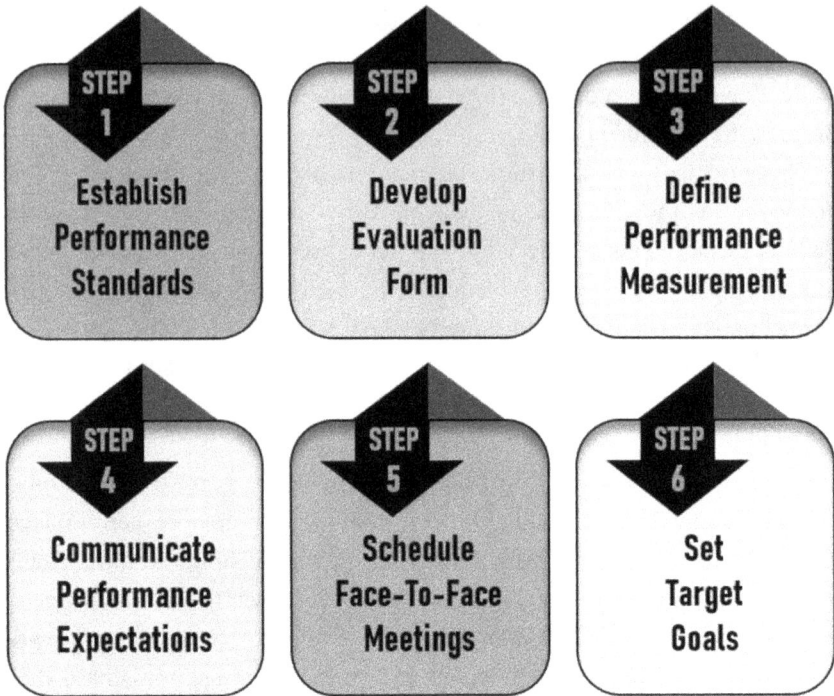

Figure 5.1 Six Essential Steps for Designing an Effective Evaluation Process. *Source*: Self-created.

SIX ESSENTIAL STEPS FOR DESIGNING AN EFFECTIVE EVALUATION PROCESS

STEP 1: Establish Performance Standards—Without standards, what are we evaluating? Not only are we left asking the question of what we are evaluating, but our people are also in the dark as to what is expected, and therefore, they are going to try to meet a standard they feel is real or simply work without accomplishing tasks to a level that is optimal for the organization. In other words, they will work all day and accomplish little, if any, of the real objectives that determine real success.

Performance standards communicate what is expected during the performance of tasks and ensure those tasks are being accomplished according to the level of quality set by the standard.

STEP 2: Develop an Effective Evaluation Form—Effective evaluation forms contain sections of relevant or required information that make the document enforceable both as a tool for employee development and as a legal support document in a wrongful termination suit. By ensuring it is effective and, more importantly, used effectively, we have taken our first steps as managers to recognize and reward good performers and protect the team and organization from poor performers. If not completed properly or not completed at all, it will have the exact opposite effect as it will certainly be introduced into evidence as exhibit A for the plaintiff.

In order to have value, it must contain the following sections or items:

- **Basic information**—this includes, but is not limited to, date, type of evaluation (quarterly, semiannual, or annual), employee name, department, position, and employee ID, along with reviewer name, title, and recommendation for retention or advancement
- **Review period**—this needs to document the time period that the evaluation is based on, and as such, the grading/ranking and evaluative statements must reflect the period covered (summative) as with all summations. While it can and should include specific events and actions that took place within the period, it should expand to include takeaways, lessons learned, and evidence of corrective actions. It is not a write-up and should not be used to double down on a specific incident that has already been addressed. What should be noted in the evaluation and what ties directly to progressive discipline is an honest assessment of corrective actions necessary for overall improvement.

    By consistently hitting our target dates for evaluations, both parties can measure progress since the previous assessment. That is the reason for interim evaluations such as quarterly and semiannual and encouraged in situations where individuals need clear improvement following incidents involving disciplinary action or serious performance concerns. Waiting six months or an entire year could prove devastating for both parties as the negative actions or performance could worsen or go unabated.
- **Rating system or scale**—This is perhaps the most important element to consider based on the huge impact it has on those being evaluated. It is where *the rubber meets the road* and what is recorded becomes permanent—at least for that period unless the reviewer changes it, which brings on a host of other problems, not to mention weakening future efforts to hold anyone accountable.

Not too long ago, a colleague shared a story of someone in their office who received a not–so-good evaluation based on the way in which they failed to perform and, more importantly, the way they disrupted the office itself by not getting along with other employees within the office and being insubordinate on a regular basis.

The assessment was accurate, and the evaluation was spot on in determining the problem, identifying the need for improvement, and scoring the performance standards objectively as they were tied to the behavior. Good job—right! Well, it was until the individual in question had a fit and stormed out of the manager's office. The next day he rewrote the evaluation and bumped up her ratings. At that point, everyone in the office was aware as she had broadcasted it. From that point on, evaluations became meaningless and the toxic atmosphere became permanent until two out of five or 40 percent of the staff left within one year of the event. And so the saga continues at least there, as the culprit remained.

This is why we need to consider the rankings we assign and commit to our assessments regardless of how emotional they are received.

Most evaluation forms used for employee evaluations fall into three categories: *scorecard*, *narrative*, and *combination*.

- **Scorecard** relies on the quantitative approach to determine whether employees can exhibit a *mastery of the concept* to achieve a high rating in various categories. This format relies on comments tied to the domain or category to ensure the rating is justified. An example would be: *Has the ability to learn and retain* related to Knowledge of Job; *or Is thorough, accurate, and neat* with respect to Quality of Work.
- **Narrative** evaluations provide a format that contains open-ended questions focused on qualitative appraisals describing how employees are attaining the standard in each domain. It provides a story with anecdotal references captured throughout the period and reflected in the evaluation to memorialize actions taken and activities completed. This opens the door for discussion, reflection, and suggestion moving forward.
- **Combination** evaluations, as the name implies, is a combined approach that captures both quantitative and qualitative information, thus providing a more holistic assessment of where individuals are with respect to the standards. This feedback within each domain expands on what drives outstanding results and focus on areas for improvement linked to unsatisfactory results. While requiring more time to complete and present, the

combination approach provides better accountability with the intent of improving performance.

STEP 3: Define Performance Measurement—Measuring job performance requires metrics that define quality, quantity, efficiency, and behaviors related to individual output and effort. While we can and should encourage team evaluations, most organizations start with and maintain a focus on individual evaluations. The use of graphic rating scales listing the traits each employee should pose provides metrics to gauge progress in attaining or maintaining such traits. Most often we find a range or scale that goes progressively from 1 being the lowest to 5 being the highest. Some companies have expanded ranges that go from 1 to 10, providing greater degrees of performance in scoring; however, the fact is there is not much difference between an "8" and "7" or "9." For someone underperforming but satisfied to get by with a "7," this can be seen as better than 50 percent or only three steps below 100 percent, whereas a "3" against a possible "5" says "Houston, - We have a problem!"

Likewise, the rating needs to be realistic and tied to a description that ensures understanding of the expectations and how to get there, as well as what is permissible or acceptable versus what constitutes unacceptable performance that, if left unchecked, can lead to nonrenewal or termination.

The worst misuse of any classification is that of "Satisfactory"—Have you ever tried to fire someone who is satisfactory? It just means they are ok and ok is all we expect, but hey, if you want to knock yourself out, go ahead and try for excellence. And by the way, in unions where salary and increment are tied to salary guides, you're going to receive the same raise as those who achieved the satisfactory ranking. How is that for motivation? It's not.

That is why we as leaders need to review existing evaluation forms and make improvements or modifications that may include throwing out the current form altogether and starting over with a better tool designed to improve all employees.

STEP 4: Communicate Performance Expectations (before, during, and after)—Describe the basic steps for conducting the evaluation, especially if this is the first time you are evaluating the individual or they are being evaluated for the first time. This should be done at the onset of the meeting to alleviate stress and concern for the unknown since those being evaluated have no idea of what to expect with a new boss or how the grading will be perceived even if the form is the same form that was used in the past.

By explaining the process, all involved start from a basis of understanding as to what is involved, what is expected, and how the evaluation is to be used. The process is much more effective when those involved are more willing to discuss issues when they understand the reason and purpose behind the evaluation. Confidentiality helps in this respect as well and should not be breached with other employees outside of HR and those in the chain of command.

This is your opportunity to initiate corrective action, if necessary, by underscoring potential disciplinary and termination procedures that should have been covered in any write-ups during the evaluation period. Remember, the comments need to be tied to the overall performance and not specific to the incident if it is the only incident in the period covered. Multiple incidents would represent a pattern and, as such, be on the table for such language.

STEP 5: Schedule a Face-to-Face Meetings—The focus here being "eye-to-eye" versus "one-to-one." During good evaluations, individuals are generally happy and look forward to the process as it will undoubtedly produce prideful moments that allow both the reviewer and the employee being reviewed ample opportunity to celebrate. However, during challenging evaluations, this is not the case. Instead, encourage supervisors and managers to team up with another manager or assistant manager or someone from HR if the evaluation is poor or bad and you expect the individual to be confrontational.

This allows individuals to read facial expressions and understand how what is written is meant by virtue of the way it is conveyed.

STEP 6: Set Target Goals—Target goals help point people in the right direction to strengthen areas for improvement while giving them something to strive for in the coming year. This is an excellent opportunity to discuss shared goals and what they would like to attempt in consideration of stretch goals. Having the individual involved in planning their goals for the upcoming period allows for a better result as they not only know what is expected but have already agreed to work on achieving it—and it's now something they want. That is motivation in action!

Chapter 6

Evaluations that Matter

Evaluations that matter are those that make a difference in the behaviors, attitudes, and outcomes of our teams. That's why we do them, that's why we need to continue to do them, and that's why they need to be authentic, honest, real, and timely. If not, then they really don't matter and that is a fact.

Want to fact-check it? Just ask a colleague or think of an instance when you yourself got called in to go over an evaluation that was bogus, meaningless, insincere, or vicious. I'm guessing they will tell you of a place they use to work, and in your case, I'm sure you've moved on from that boss or you're just waiting for the opportunity to leave or wish them well as they quit, retire, or get, as we covered in chapter 5, terminated.

"The main objective of performance appraisals is to measure and improve the performance of employees and increase their future potential and value to the company. Other objectives include providing feedback, improving communication, understanding training needs, clarifying roles and responsibilities and determining how to allocate rewards."[1]

Driven by a vision of success where organizations perform at their peak requires the empowerment of managers to incorporate accountability into the evaluation while engaging employees through honest feedback and ownership of their performance and responsibilities. This is accomplished by providing evaluation tools that lead the way to better performance, thus achieving that success by managing talent and shedding those who are incompetent or consistently underperforming. Talent management requires action in support of that vision to achieve the kind of success companies and organizations are in search of, and evaluations are the vehicle to get us there.

In a recent article I shared on Twitter titled "17 Mind-blowing Statistics on Performance Reviews and Employee Engagement"[2] that point was captured in the following paragraphs:

> Constructive feedback is vital to an employee's ongoing development. From A Players to under-performers, and everything in between, employees need timely, specific, and helpful feedback to reach their full potential. Positive feedback helps build confidence, while constructive criticism clarifies expectations and allows people to learn from their mistakes.

> In the current workplace, the annual performance review isn't your only opportunity to tell your employees what's working and what's not. 96% of employees say that they want to hear feedback regularly. Daniel Pink, a Washington D.C.-based author says, "There's no way to get better at something you only hear about once a year."

Survey Monkey, a global leader in online survey tools boasting twenty million questions answered daily, points out, "Regular performance reviews—of individuals, teams, and managers—can give you timely insight into the health of the very heart of your company: Your employees. Traditional employee surveys conducted by human resources departments allow management to gather the business crucial feedback. However, a focused employee self-evaluation allows for management and their workforce to engage in a helpful dialogue about career development and goals"[3]

Just completing the evaluation does not make it effective, and if done poorly can cause damage to the individual and, by extension, the team. Sub-par evaluations are those improperly prepared or poorly delivered or a combination of both. An individual can receive a poor or bad evaluation but that is not the same thing as an evaluation that is done poorly. When this happens, the individual becomes less motivated if they feel they are not appreciated, are misrepresented, or feel the evaluation is used to hurt their opportunity for advancement or consideration of a meaningful raise.

Often managers who commit these blunders are doing so because they are unprepared, lack the details of the individual's performance, are missing notes and specific examples, missed out on the observations, and now try to hurry the process or harbor resentment of the task. In a survey conducted by Quantum Workplace, "One in five employees is not confident their manager will provide regular, constructive feedback."[4]

UC Davis recognizes the importance of observations, and the value placed on them can be found on their HR website, chocked full of resources to aid managers in their efforts. The "call-to-action" informs managers that they should observe employees' performance and provide feedback once performance objectives and standards have been established.

> You have a responsibility to recognize and reinforce strong performance by an employee, and identify and encourage improvement where it is needed. You provide informal feedback almost every day. By observing and providing detailed feedback, you play a critical role in the employee's continued success and motivation to meet performance expectations.[5]

Their performance appraisal system dubbed UCPath is available to managers through their HR portal containing links to additional training content and other helpful guides and info. As the name implies, a "path" for an effective evaluation process is laid out to guide the manager and benefit the employee on the journey.

In education we place a premium on directional guidance referred to as "pathways" to ensure our students make the proper connections in order to navigate academic programs and learning experiences needed to ensure graduation.

These learning pathways are personalized and multiple to ensure everyone's success. When it comes to evaluations, we need to think along those lines of developing both *individual* and *multiple pathways* to enhance and improve performance in order to attain better results for the individual while strengthening the team. Teams get stronger one member at a time. Each individual's success represents a win for the team and those wins propel our teams forward into achieving greater accomplishments. In this case, instead of "taking one for the team," we are "making one for the team" and everyone wins!

So let's dig deeper—it's time to get into the details. In the last chapter, we covered the evaluation process and how to improve it. Now let's focus on elements that make the process of evaluating staff stronger that include performance notes, evaluation methods, performance reviews, feedback, and goal setting (figure 6.1).

Elements of a Strong Evaluation Process

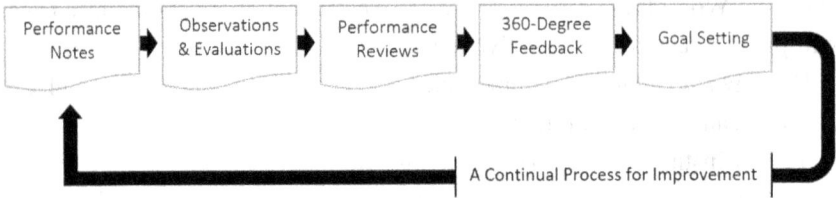

Figure 6.1   Elements of a Strong Evaluation Process. *Source*: Self-created.

As you can see by the directional arrows, it is systematic and continuous in order to be effective and remain constant. From gathering performance notes to conducting observations and evaluations, we continue to record performance to reinforce our expectations and deliver effective guidance in our performance reviews. 360-degree feedback provides us with a holistic picture of the performance and its impact on operations inside and outside of the department or group. All of this provides better opportunity for goal setting that is targeted and focused on the feedback.

Notice *performance reviews* are at the center of our diagram. While the process is continuous, it is the performance review stage that serves as the culmination of all the notes, observations, and evaluations to set the stage for the big discussions that will shape our teams according to each member in a one-on-one style that is individualized with the overall team in mind. That is how we enrich our team performance by ensuring all members of the team are performing at the top of their game. As such we need to concern ourselves with how to conduct performance reviews in a way that makes them as effective as they are intended to be, in short—giving them value.

Let's start by examining ways to improve the richness of data to shape the narrative and support the rankings assigned to the scale. In order to ensure we have valid data, concrete examples, and pin-point recommendations to drive discussion, increase awareness, and improve performance, we need to record actions and events during the period to create a look back that accurately captures the performance during that period.

This is accomplished through one-on-ones (individual observations and evaluations) and team reviews (group evaluations) along with strong PD (professional development) and group activities, exercises and retreats.

So again how do we actually improve our preparation for the big discussions that matter? Here are a couple of quick and effective methods to improve our ability to gather data and incorporate sample material from observations that will strengthen those evaluations to capture true performance. Once we have mastered this task, our evaluations will be better, more authentic, and more meaningful.

TIPS TO HELP YOU PREPARE
PERFORMANCE EVALUATIONS

- **Anecdotal Records**

Anecdotal records offer a detailed description of behaviors that are witnessed. They are nothing more than quick notes that capture what already took place. Notes can help us by becoming an effective memory aid to capture the highlights or lowlights of the event or events that have already transpired. If you are not doing this already, you are missing out on an easy and effective way to document happenings while they are fresh in your mind. As a leader, this gives you an opportunity to provide instant feedback while prepping for the summative evaluation to come.

Focus on the key takeaways to provide clear instruction as to what is good and should be repeated versus what should be avoided or discouraged. Over time, a collection of anecdotal records provides a great deal of information to draw from in crafting a detailed observation that provides valuable feedback.

- **Jotting Notes**

Whether your preference is to go "old-school" (pad and pen) or embrace eNotes with the use of devices and apps, jotting down notes helps us track performance throughout the evaluation period. This is simply keeping track of events related to the observations—date, time, place along with which performance standards were covered or missed.

Does anyone have a pen? Damn, where is my pad?—Spot evaluation opportunities pop up quickly leaving us unprepared for formal assessments; however, one quick and easy tool that everyone has in their possession these days is the smartphone, and it can be highly effective in jotting down notes through your notes app or look at installing one of these: OneNote, Evernote, Material Notes, Google Keep, Simplenote, or Keep My Notes all featured by TechRadar, as *Best Note Keeping Apps for 2020.*[6]

A major feature of these apps is the ability to move the notes to your email and upload the content into your documents to assist with the narrative. Many of the apps update across all your devices automatically and in real time. There's no "sync" button: It just works. Formatting options allow you to speak (voice-to-text), write, preview, and publish your notes. Best of all you have a record that you can go back to with respect to actual date and time versus the days of digging through an organizer or pocket calendar. Likewise, a picture is worth 1,000 words—how about a picture of the actual words themselves. Pictures are a great reference tool and every smartphone comes with a high-quality camera thus allowing for quick documentation of the effort.

• **Work Samples**

Next time you see a sample of work that reflects the standards you are looking for from the employee in question, grab it and put into a folder for later. When it comes time to evaluate the employee, you will have actual work product to refer to in the discussion and attachment support for inclusion in the comments. Work samples serve as concrete illustrations of what the individual is capable of producing. Work samples include correspondence, spreadsheets, reports, analysis, or other related documents to their position and responsibilities.

Once you have notes and samples in hand, you are prepared and ready to tackle the evaluation with credible illustrations of their performance from the evaluations. While there are many different methods available and each has their own Pros/Cons, you will achieve better results regardless of which method you choose. Here are some of the most common methods to consider.

OBSERVATION METHODS FOR EFFECTIVE EVALUATIONS

• **360-Degree Employee Evaluation**

This method assesses your person's skills, behavior, and impact on the rest of the team. Since it's anonymous it provides unfettered feedback and perspectives that could go unaddressed. Using 360-degree feedback evaluations strengthens teams as they explore impacts across department lines and within entire work flows. "360 feedback doesn't actually focus on performance, but rather on all aspects that can be attributed to an employee's behavior. In this way it can help the person improve their interactions, their communication, and in the end, their job performance."[7]

- **Objectives and Metrics**

  Management by Objectives (MBO) utilizes objectives and metrics to determine whether individuals are successful in meeting the needs of the organization by attainment of goals and objectives. Metrics are quick indicators to measure progress in relationship to those goals. Job descriptions entail unique responsibilities, goals, and objectives, and metrics allow us to gauge progress in order to give feedback with respect to those goals during the period in which they are being evaluated. Goals can encompass anything from operations to success rates, task completion or other performance that can be measured like sales, customer satisfaction, overall quality, and increased net worth. Performance metrics vary depending on the industry.

  This method is highly effective in devolving talent as it permits employers to customize the approach and link performance to the job goals outlined in the job descriptions. Keep in mind this is also an opportunity to review and modify existing job descriptions to keep them relevant and effective.

- **Self-Evaluation**

  This method engages employees by requiring them to rate themselves with multiple choice and open-ended questions to seriously consider their level of performance and areas they can improve. By assessing their own work performance, it gives the rater a better insight into where the employee believes their strengths and weaknesses are in relationship to what they need to do to perform properly. This can be a helpful way to dive into those difficult conversations that need to happen for true improvement with respect to weaknesses or deficiencies yet also allows for positive reinforcement of strengths and skills that benefit the team.

  Self-evaluation puts ownership on the employee to perform an honest assessment of how they are doing, and let's be honest, all individuals are different. While some are harder on themselves than others, there are those who believe they are doing great—yet when the manager's assessment comes out, they look nothing alike. This could be seen as a con; however, it instantly shows the disconnect which is now in writing and therefore should become the beginning of a corrective action plan and form the basis for personal goal setting in a PIP (Personal Improvement Plan) to gain the necessary improvement for the individual and the team.

Whether you are using an actual self-evaluation form or not, every evaluation should contain an opportunity for the person being evaluated to be reflective and ready to openly discuss behaviors that need to be addressed and deficiencies that require improvement. Without an honest and open dialog, these issues go unaddressed even if they are recorded as the individual may not fully understand what the issue(s) are and how to go about improving them. Best advice is to be honest, direct, and concerned. Demonstrating true care and concern goes a long way in addressing issues that need to be addressed. Don't let them go unspoken; the result will just be more of the same and the impact of the poor performance will only be greater. Remember, saying nothing says it is ok—and it's not.

- **Graphic Rating Scale**

As touched on earlier, this is perhaps the most common performance evaluation method in use today as it is quick, categorized, and instant with respect to score. Basically a report card that captures how well individuals measure up against predetermined aspects of performance that indicate where the individual is along the scale from needs improvement to outstanding or excellent.

The challenge with this type of evaluation method is that lack of depth with respect to scale as many times a person falls between two numbers on the scale as their performance falls somewhere in between, often leaning more toward one of the numbers. This is where the narrative is a must to support and explain the number value selected. Even when someone is performing at a high level and achieves the top rating, they need to know why in order to maintain those actions moving forward.

- **Developmental Checklist**

This method allows manager to measure attributes, developmental progress, and skills against a checklist of performance categories, listing expected behavioral qualities and skills to succeed in the position.

Developmental checklists provide a basic overview within major components of the performance measures of a job and allow the manager to rate the employee to determine if they have met or exceeded the expectation or standard. This is an opportunity to identify areas in need of improvement where the individual has failed to meet the standard. Put in a more positive way, "Where the individual has *not yet*"[8] met the standard. The later statement shows hope and gives an expectation that progress will come.

- **Critical Incident Performance Appraisal**

  This method utilizes Key Performance Indicators (KPI) as metrics tied to benchmarks the organization or business monitors to ensure success. More detailed and usually tied to an employee online management tool, it allows managers and employees to track performance against targets and expectations that are considered a critical path to success.

  In sales, for instance, many of the KPIs would be tied to actual sales production for a period in question such as monthly, quarterly, and annual.

  The CI method measures both performance and behaviors linked to performance metrics. Like the other methods, supportive evidence is found in records, noting both positive and negative impacts on operations, departments, and teams.

THINGS TO AVOID IN WRITING EVALUATIONS

Evaluations that are poorly written, badly constructed, or deficient are ones that lack honesty in assessing bad behaviors or simply fail to capture specific areas of performance that need improvement.

Here are seven examples to avoid when writing evaluations:

1 THE ROLLER COASTER EVALUATION—Up and down, going from the best to the worst and back up again. Reminiscent of ABC's Wide World of Sports, the thrill of victory, and the agony of defeat all neatly packaged into one evaluation.

   Problem—Lacks consistency and appears exaggerative thus lacking validity.

2 THE LONG OVERDUE EVALUATION—Evaluations need to be timely and relevant.

   Problem—Missing timelines allows poor performance to go unchecked and undocumented. At the same time good performance is left unrecognized and unrewarded

3 THE PENCIL WHIP—Signified by a lack of effort they become meaningless. Completed quickly and without thought or just copied over from prior evaluations. The evaluee is left feeling it doesn't matter, allowing poor performers to continue and good performers to lose interest.

   Problem—Narrative not consistent with actual performance.

4 THE ABSENT EVALUATION—It's not there. When you search the drive or filing cabinet, it cannot be found. Either it never happened or it was not recorded.

Problem—Lack of support for progressive discipline. Facts are lost and we are back to square one in documenting poor performance if a decision was made to terminate based on the poor performance. Also this is bad for the good employees who worked hard and now feel unappreciated and taken for granted.

5 THE LOPSIDED EVALUATION—Weighted too heavily on either end of the period or based on the last few months due to a lack of preparation throughout the period, it is not fair or balanced.

Problem—These type of evaluations become narrow in focus and are not representative of a summative evaluation. They can appear vindictive if based on a particular incident that was already addressed. In this case, they can be seen as retaliatory especially if the focus is only on negatives.

6 THE UNTOUCHABLE EVALUATION—We are talking *"walks on water."* You're it and no room for improvement, aka "I got this job on lockdown and I'm taking it easy from here on out." As good as anyone is, there is always room for improvement or a need to set higher goals.

Problem—These types of evaluations can leave some employees feeling they should either *"dial it back"* or they may begin to feel under compensated producing thoughts like *"Should I be getting more money? What am I doing here? or I should be running this place."*

7 THE FIRE BRAND EVALUATION—Marked by an overly harsh evaluation leaving the evaluee feeling *"branded for life"* or at least till the next evaluation.

Problem—Evaluations that are too harsh undermine your efforts for corrective action as the *reflection opportunity* is lost by the individual who can become discouraged, angry, or outraged. These feelings can lead to discouragement, *"Why try, I'm done,"* or blocking—refusing to see the issue because of the outrage, or in the worst case, retaliation in the form of passive aggressive behavior.

While some managers favor benevolence over responsibility, culminating in an evaluation that is not reflective of actual performance, the problem they cause goes much deeper. Missing out on a chance to affect performance is a wasted opportunity and a waste of time—but doing damage by providing the grounds for a lawsuit is far worse.

Although evaluations are designed to provide managers with a tool to identify, shape, and improve performance, they become evidentiary records in support of progressive discipline. While they are confidential in nature, they are discoverable, "Whether personnel records are admissible into evidence is a different issue than whether they are discoverable, and this will always be a fact-intensive inquiry."[9] Discovery goes both ways and poorly written evaluations can be used by plaintiff's counsel as evidence to overturn terminations.

Anyone with considerable time spent in the workforce can no doubt recall a situation where management was delinquent in documenting and correcting behaviors of a problem employee, yet when it appeared to be the *right time*, they walked the individual out only to receive a "wrongful termination" suit weeks later.

This was the case involving a Michigan man who in 2010 was fired from his position at St. Mary's Surgical Services in Grand Rapids based on his inability to control inventory and the subsequent fiscal loss experienced by the hospital. Subordinates had also made several allegations of unprofessionalism and favoritism in numerous complaints filed with superiors.

The termination took place on May 10, a Monday; twelve weeks later on another Monday, August 9, the plaintiff (T. Fuhr) filed a one-count complaint, alleging that his termination was due to a complaint he filed with the US attorney's office regarding overbilling and as such constituted a violation of the Whistle Blower Protection Act (WPA).

The alleged overbilling complaint Fuhr reported filing was not substantiated and, according to Fuhr's own testimony, would have happened after the termination.

Part of the problem for St. Mary's was that Fuhr had two excellent evaluations in the two years prior to the termination, stating that he had met or exceeded the standards for his position in all categories. Also there was a damaging email introduced into evidence in support of the plaintiff—the hospital's CEO, Phil McCorkle, sent an email to Tom Karel, the hospital's vice president. The email stated, in relevant part:

Steve [Pirog] said that [plaintiff] . . . is on the way out and that Amy Moored from finance will be assigned to get the OR inventory corrected.[10]

While the judge granted a summary judgment to the defendants (St. Mary's) on March 30, 2012, the case was appealed and overturned a year later by the Michigan Court of Appeals in favor of the plaintiff (Todd Fuhr). That finding was challenged on appeal by the defendant Trinity Health-Michigan and eventually reversed by the Michigan Supreme Court on October 2, 2013, via a REVERSE judgment of the Court of Appeals, for the reasons stated in the Court of Appeals dissenting opinion. As such the Supreme Court of Michigan reinstated the March 30, 2012, order of the Kent Circuit Court granting summary disposition to the defendants (St. Mary's).

So two years and three months later and after a considerable amount paid in legal costs including discovery, depositions, litigation, and court fees, St. Mary's Hospital prevailed when they could have simply avoided the cost of the suit and the time spent defending it by completing accurate evaluations and following a clear policy on dismissal.

Another takeaway here and everywhere: *the "e" in email stands for evidence!* Lessons learned the hard way in business come at a cost and sometimes that cost is unrecoverable, even when insurance comes into play—the payout still costs you beyond your deductible as it goes against your experience. Too many claims and you may find your rates jacked up or worse—that you are being dropped from your carrier seen as a liability.

In a similar situation we had an employee who was disruptive, ineffective, and insubordinate. The individual had been counseled, written up, and sat down with HR, yet the behaviors continued and became more disruptive to coworkers. Once the individual started using words like "hostile work environment," we knew it was time to act and act swiftly. We consulted our labor attorney and got the following opinion: "Terminate the employment immediately—the good news, you have just ended your liability from this point forward."

In short, once a decision is made to terminate an employee, make sure it is supported by facts and carried out swiftly in accordance with your HR policy on termination. If you don't have procedures for termination covered in the policy, that's the first thing you need to resolve.

Part III

TAKING TEAM PERFORMANCE
TO THE NEXT LEVEL

Chapter 7

Rewarding Individual Performance

Taking team performance to the next level starts by ensuring those on the team are valued in ways that are thoughtful, meaningful, and personalized. This is different from incentives or rewards programs tied to quotas or sales goals. Again money is not the only carrot and gift cards, while appreciated, are short in duration and typically small in value; yet their impact lingers—why? Not because of the monetary value, but more the thought that resonates with individuals and the joy of being appreciated. "In a highly competitive marketplace, companies need to up the ante to attract the best workers. Fair salaries and medical benefits are no longer enough to attract workers to a new organization. It all comes down to offering certain perks and benefits that truly resonate with the worker of today."[1]

I shared an article recently on Twitter and LinkedIn written by Ben Goldstein titled, "8 Ways to Retain your Top Sales Reps (After They've Gotten Their Bonuses)"; what grabbed my attention was the subtext, the part in parenthesis, after they've gotten their bonuses. Without even reading it, I liked the fact that he hit on a popular theme—*that money isn't always the motivator to keep people engaged* and *keep people from leaving*. That doesn't mean money doesn't matter; without a competitive salary and bonus program in the world of sales, you will likely see quicker turnover with top performers. Not only is it costly; it expends resources covered in the first part of this book—gathering talent.

So once this is straightened out and you find your compensation package is competitive, you need to go beyond the expected and start creating value add for the individual. A good start is to recognize employees as team members and treat them accordingly since they make us productive and without them we fail.

Goldstein opens with a picture of an executive approaching a directional signpost pointing the way toward four chief desires that all top performers seek: purpose, engagement, opportunity, and growth. Whether you're in sales or any line of work that offers a career path, if you're motivated and looking to achieve and succeed, you are banking on these prospects and organizations that can supply them are where you want to be and most likely where you will stay longer. According to the US Bureau of Labor Statistics, the median number of years that wage and salary workers had been with their current employer was 4.1 years in January 2020, down slightly from 4.2 years in January 2018.[2]

I grew up in an era of "job-for-life"—a job that you could stay in with a company or organization that offered the classic *"mailroom to boardroom"* opportunity or starting on nights and working your way to days then eventually getting promoted to foreman or department head and in due course walk out with a pension, a lifetime of memories, and a gold watch commemorating forty years or more with the same employer. Today, it's unheard of or better yet unthought-of as most individuals in the labor market recognize that greater advancement is typically gained by moving from one company to another in order to get higher wages, better accommodations such as increased PTO and better health-care coverage. Pensions are another thing of the past as more and more employees and employers count on 401k's and similar individual retirement accounts that are portable.

So how do some organizations best others in becoming the *Best Companies to Work for*? For one, they focus as much on *how they make their members feel by providing a true sense of care and commitment* as they do on being profitable in their markets. Their success is marked by rankings and reports detailing how these companies outperform competitors and achieve the goal of recognizing, growing, and attracting talent that stays and produces while enjoying the challenge and experiences they share as part of great teams.

Great Place to Work® is the global authority on workplace culture. They lead the industry in data mining by surveying more than 100 million employees around the world and using that data gain deep insights into what makes a great workplace. The rigor associated with their trademarked data-based model—the Work Trust Model™—has been in practice since 1992.[3] The model centers on Credibility, Respect, Pride, Camaraderie, and Fairness. Sounds simple, yet there are still companies and organizations that miss the mark in many of these core areas. The group at Great Place puts the employee at the heart of their model and use it to power their Trust Index Survey™ and Culture Management platform producing annual rankings in reports that include

- WORLD'S BEST WORKPLACES™
- BEST WORKPLACES FOR WOMEN™
- PEOPLE COMPANIES THAT CARE
- BEST WORKPLACES FOR MILLENNIALS
- FORTUNE 100 BEST COMPANIES TO WORK FOR

What Great Places to Work recognizes and points out in the data uncovered in their reports is that *how you make your members feel* directly correlates to *why they want to be on your team.* Look at Hilton Hotel & Resorts, a leader in the hospitality industry voted #1 in Fortune 100 Best Companies to Work For® 2020 and #3 for best workplaces in the world in 2020 despite the enormous challenges of COVID-19. When you go on their website in search of opportunities, you are greeted by a search bar inviting you to *"Search for your dream job"* along with a bolded *call-to-action* stating, "Join the Hilton Talent Community," underscoring the fact that they are after all a talent organization—and they have room for you. As pointed out in the report, *"Even as it laid off and furloughed workers, Hilton's leaders came up with novel ways to support employees and help them land jobs elsewhere. It also got creative about using empty hotel rooms to house medical professionals on the pandemic frontlines."*[4]

When people have purpose, they have meaning.

This is what gets them up every day with a renewed sense of value because they belong to something bigger than themselves, and they look forward to showcasing their talents and applying their skills as part of a team. I often refer to the work of Rick Warren with his groundbreaking book *The Purpose Driven Life*, which asks the most basic question everyone faces in life, "Why am I here?" While the book is intended to answer a life-message, it poses a great question that each of us has asked about our *work life* in the same way at some point or another. Typically, it comes up during periods of high stress, annoyance, concern for the future of the organization, or when you're simply overwhelmed. In contrast, people who love their work and, more importantly, where they work are less likely to ask this question as it becomes self-evident in their attitude and performance regardless of the challenges they encounter or the stressors that come with the job they manage. So how do we give them purpose? Start by giving them meaning.

The following are just a handful of ideas that can easily foster a culture of *purpose, engagement, opportunity,* and *growth* for team members at all levels:

- Include your team members in planning through scheduled discussion group meetings. These can be weekly, bi-monthly, or monthly and can be done informally by connecting them to a fun activity such as a coffee break and afternoon break. I started this years ago, and my staff still appreciates the time, attention, and focus on what we do as a group. Gaining a better understanding of what others are doing for the team and how their contributions help goes a long way in providing them with a high-level view to see the big picture. Giving them opportunities to provide updates on tasks they are completing and time to share their thoughts and suggestions to improve overall performance empowers them and keeps them engaged.

- Allow junior managers and supervisors to present at cabinet or high-level meetings or simply accompany senior managers from time to time depending on the topics being discussed at higher-level meetings. In addition to the appreciated exposure, they gain valuable insights, unique perspectives on management, and a better understanding of executive roles and responsibilities. This is especially evidenced in high-performing organizations that value the development of team members by broadening their knowledge and spotlighting their talents.

- Bring along administrative assistants to professional trainings outside of the organization that fall within their areas of responsibility. Take insurance, for instance, you probably have an administrative assistant or secretary handling clerical functions like coordination of claims, dealing with policy renewals, billings, and other tasks associated with your property casualty lines of coverage. Odds are they spend a considerable amount of time throughout the year on the phone with providers, brokers, and representatives regarding those claims, policies, and associated cases. When the opportunity presents itself, take them to one of the trainings at your level or, better yet, to a quarterly or annual board meeting. Include your team members whenever possible; including them at a lunch with your broker gives them a sense of worth and a feeling of appreciation that goes well beyond a gift card or a pat on the back.

- Spotlight the efforts of your team members and give them the credit they deserve by acknowledging their work and the *value-add* they bring to the team with your superiors. One easy way to do this is share author rights in the footer of spreadsheets or on the cover of reports. If they provide you with a document that they did 100 percent of the work on, let their name stand alone.

- Encourage members of your team to push for personal growth by enrolling in higher education, pursuing graduate degrees, obtaining licenses, or attending leadership courses. Whenever one succeeds, we all succeed and sharing in someone's success is what leadership development is all about. The pride that is shared and the knowledge that is given provide purpose for both the protégé and the mentor. Learning is a lifelong journey, and having the opportunity to serve as a guide in developing talent is one of the most purposeful enrichments an organization can provide to its top leaders.

- Cross-training is one of the best ways to increase engagement by allowing individuals to gain knowledge in new areas of responsibilities and at the same time increase their personal worth. Besides the fact that it just makes good sense in retaining the ability to manage operations should key individuals go out on an unexpected absence or just miss a few days during a critical time period. Likewise, it allows team members to gain a better perspective on the overall operation and get to know other team members better. In order for this to work effectively, it needs to be communicated as to the "why" and supervised to ensure the training is authentic and effective. Like anything that requires planning, it must be done ahead of the crisis in order to have value and tested to ensure it is effective when needed.

Beyond these opportunities, professional development remains one of the best ways to engage and reward individual performance and identify future leaders by giving them an opportunity to attend regional, state, and national conferences that focus on disciplines related to their areas of impact.

Conferences are more than just exciting trips to trendy destinations; they provide growth opportunities, presentation opportunities, and networking opportunities in ways that are as impactful as they are memorable. Often times this becomes a perk for the members; however, a coup for the organization as they not only ensure their best and brightest stay engaged and content, but also become the benefactors of the learned knowledge and cutting edge perspective on what's new, relevant, and working in the industry.

While these activities provide occasions to recognize and reward individuals, they have a larger impact on employee engagement as they are the type of perks and benefits that employees begin looking forward to and consider part of their package adding to their longevity.

Great companies like Hilton are considered great by their employees because they are seen as caring for them as much as the bottom line. Hilton's management team in turn values the importance of their personnel and understands the significance of *happiness* to the company's success as that *happiness* translates into employees who are committed and attentive as they cheerfully greet and assist guests in ways that make them feel valued, thus enriching their experience.

Want to find another example of a great company that gets it—when it comes to recognizing and rewarding their employees, Dollar General is a true standout earning their second consecutive ranking of #1 by Training Magazine in their annual Top 125 Organizations. These are organizations that excelled at employee training and development in the last year. The 2019 list put Dollar General into a special category—as they are set to be inducted into the Training Top 10 Hall of Fame in 2021 after finishing in the Top 10 for four consecutive years.[5]

What stands out with this Tennessee-based retailer is their commitment to their training for team members by ensuring quality training of over 140,000 employees annually with approximately 12,000 store managers promoted from within, while, at the same time, posting an impressive 56 percent of job openings filled by internal candidates and 44 percent of new hires coming as referrals from current employees.[6]

Dollar General's Senior Vice President and Chief People Officer Kathy Reardon refers to their mission of "Serving Others" that has guided the company since its founding in 1939 as a family-owned business called J. L. Turner and Son in Scottsville, Kentucky. What makes Dollar General such a great example is their commitment to pathways to education and career growth opportunities utilizing what she proudly refers to as "Best-in-class, award-winning training and development programs."[7]

> Our employees are our competitive advantage, and we are committed to providing opportunities to enhance and develop their talents, engage our teams, and celebrate continued career advancement with the organization.—Kathy Reardon, Senior VP, CPO Dollar General 2019

Fortune 500 also recognized Dollar General in their 2020 rankings just outside the Top 100 of their list, putting the retailer at #112, noting, "The discount retailer, which calls itself the country's 'largest small box retailer,' operates more than 15,000 stores in forty-four states and is headquartered in Goodlettsville, Tenn."[8] As of January 31, 2020, that count has jumped to an impressive 16,278 stores and has become one of the most profitable stores in the rural United States with sales of $27.8 billion in 2019.[9]

CEO Tod J. Vasos opens the Annual Report with a welcome greeting to fellow shareholders, customers, and employees with highlights and strong results recognizing 2019 as a pivotal year for their long-term strategic initiatives centered on the company's four key operating priorities: (1) driving profitable sales growth, (2) capturing growth opportunities, (3) leveraging and reinforcing their position as a low-cost operator, and (4) investing in their people as a competitive advantage.[10] It is this fourth priority (*employee investment*) that continues to make the company profitable as they retain their talent who in turn seeks avenues of growth to management and the ability to allow the company to expand with new locations that are run by experienced managers. That commitment is captured in the remarks Vasos penned as follows:

> *"Investing in our people as a competitive advantage: The investments we have made in our people delivered benefits again in 2019 as we saw our lowest store manager turnover on record. We continue to provide world-class training opportunities for our people, and we believe the opportunity to start and develop a career with a growing retailer is a competitive advantage."*[11]

What's amazing is the growth the company has had in the past thirteen years doubling the number of stores nationwide by 98.7 percent from 8,194 stores in 2007 to 16,278 stores in 2019.[12]

Take a ride outside any major city or suburb and you are sure to find a clean, hassle-free convenient discount retail store with a big yellow sign across the front, "DOLLAR GENERAL" with their mantra of offering quality brands at low prices. The key to their success is in large part due to the employees inside who continue to be recognized and rewarded for their performance. That recognition goes beyond the actual stores and continues to be enjoyed by their executive team members in performance incentives that include cash and stock options tied to earnings. At Dollar General, everyone wins and it's quite an army.

Recognizing and rewarding members of any team will always produce positive results gaining loyalty, appreciation, dedication, and longevity.

Chapter 8

Boosting Team Performance

Even in tough times, we need to find ways to boost our team's performance in order to ensure we are maximizing our opportunities and delivering on our promises to our clients, stakeholders, and those we are responsible for—those in our charge and our members. Asking more from our members at a time when they are dealing with more than their fair share of personal challenges, concerns, and fears with the arrival of COVID-19 adds another layer of challenge to what must be done in spite of this or any pandemic or crisis.

I recently participated in a Zoom meeting with colleagues from across the country to discuss the 2021 editorial calendar for School Business Affairs, an international publication provided by ASBO International based in Ashburn, VA.

While we discussed and debated articles related to the topics based on monthly selections for the magazine, we did, as has been our practice, discuss the relevance of current events and how they continue to shape our world and impact our communities.

Not surprisingly, the conversations continued to veer in the direction of COVID-19. From which school districts were delivering in-person instruction versus remote learning; maintaining social distancing requirements; challenges with contact tracing; how we were handling operational disruptions like plummeting sales from foodservice; to how we were able to support, inspire, and direct our teams during the greatest challenge of our lifetime. Likewise, the considerable discussion focused on the degree of impact COVID-19 should have in shaping those articles for 2021 as it all but dominated 2020; and whether we should begin to move on in anticipation of the post-COVID-19 world we desperately await.

The next morning, while thinking of our decision to continue to consider the impact of COVID-19 by incorporating elements that fit into articles to generate support for our member's needs over the next year, it became clear that we made a good decision. The decision to continue to offer support based on the needs of our readership was exemplified in a post I read that morning by another colleague on LinkedIn titled The Principal Is Not Ok.

> *I know Covid is hard on my students, families, staff and teachers, and community. But running a school right now feels impossible and thankless.*
> *I have to be Strong, Positive and Brave for everyone. I'm exhausted. I had to just tell someone. . . . The Principal is not okay.*

The comments of the challenged principal served to underscore the sentiment shared by the group: that while we need to look forward, we need to consider the impact this is currently still having on leaders and organizations, not to mention the social-emotional toll on our students. Although its impact may be considered short-term, the long-term effects will be with us for the foreseeable future. While the themes for each month center on specific issues, they are connected by their focus on teams and our ability to provide those teams with knowledge, strategies, and resources to boost their performance.

As leaders of school districts that include the greater St. Louis area, Chicago suburbs, Norman, Oklahoma, NJ/NY Metro, Philadelphia and Allentown PA, Arlington, VA, and Iowa Farmlands, we found strength and resilience in moving beyond the crisis to frame the content needed to move teams forward as we all fight the pandemic. In a broader sense, our meeting provided the boost we needed as individual organizations to fuel the drive of our stakeholders—the largest network of school business officials in the world.

2020 has become the lost year for many teams and organizations/companies experiencing wide-scale closures in various industries, shortened or canceled sports seasons, shutdowns in the art and entertainment field, and shrinking or lost sales for many retailers and restaurants. At the same time, we witnessed large gains for technology companies, fast food restaurants with drive-thru capability, and restaurants capable of offering takeout.

Gone with the year of shutdowns were conferences, traveling, vacations, business trips, in-person meetings, annual outings, large gatherings, parties, and more. What replaced this loss was online video conferencing software solutions like ClickMeeting, Zoom, GoToMeeting, Webex, and others and a new kind of office experience for millions of workers called "The Home Office."

Like its namesake, spaces in our homes became transformed into remote office location studios to improve the audio and visual experience as teachers turned living rooms into classrooms, and dining rooms became the backdrop for payroll, purchase order processing, and team meetings. Individuals fortunate to have actual office space in their homes now faced the task of cleaning up and cleaning out areas to reflect the professional setting needed to host webinars, board meetings, and public meetings.

The need to move forward continued on many fronts despite the impending fear of outside contact, especially in the early months of the shutdown (March–May). While the concerns gradually lifted and shifted by the summer, the need to "keep our distance" remained in place, putting a continued challenge and strain on companies and their employees. As we drew closer to the end of the year, the restrictions only tightened once more as "closures" worldwide ramped up, shutting down restaurants, closing schools, and ending many businesses that couldn't handle the second wave of restrictions and closures.

Those restrictions under executive orders issued by governors across the country pushed workers and companies backward as they were again remanded to their homes resulting in a resurgence of work from home for those equipped and mass layoffs, furloughs, or shutdowns for others just before the holidays.

At a time when people need the closeness of family and the ability to celebrate and share their faith through meals, family gatherings, church, and other community events and groups, they are left separated and further from the ability to socialize. People reported being "Zoom-fatigued" at work and missing the connections through group activities and experiences like conference attendance and training that boost team spirit and overall performance.

So, how do companies and organizations address this need and broader needs for their teams? How do they accomplish it while grappling with the challenges of this or any pandemic? Especially given that it threatens the livelihood of the economy and perhaps the business itself! Telling them to brace for the "new normal" is not an acceptable response.

There is a clear difference between adapting and improvising and taking extra care of your teams during a crisis. Adapting to changing conditions to stay afloat and relevant in the world of business is about the needs of the company or organization. Taking extra care of your teams involves humanizing your approach, supplying additional resources, and adding check-ins to ensure they are managing outside of work as well as in work.

What is at stake, and what matters most, is how we maintain that support and connection for our teams. Support will ensure our team(s) get the care they need in the midst of what has become the greatest challenge of our generation, akin to the Spanish Flu of 1918 or the Great Depression of the 1930s. It has become, as one friend put it, "our greatest generation moment."

Boosting team performance in the middle of a pandemic is a little more challenging than during normal times, but innovative leaders and forward-thinking companies always find ways to meet those challenges and emerge stronger from the experience. Fostering a sentiment *of apart—but not alone*—reinforces the notion of unity and a message of hope.

Successful companies understand this and have already implemented strategies designed to manage and stay ahead of the closures until the economy rebounds—and it will. They include

1. **Providing Greater Flexibility**—"Before the pandemic, only about 5% of the U.S. workforce worked from home on a regular basis."[1] As more and more companies look to continue operations during the pandemic, their stance on allowing employees to work from home has transitioned from a decision to a requirement with portable devices being issued and conference software being installed.

    The existence of online modern enterprise video communications solutions with reliable cloud platforms for video and audio conferencing, chat, and webinars, and their ease of use has provided an option for work at home that did not exist a decade ago. Now a variety of industries from education to health care are able to capitalize on the progress made to enable their workers to participate in online meetings, chats, use breakout rooms, collaborate in workspaces, answer and return office calls through their computers, and participate in video webinars with easy-to-use features that are part of the training.

It is expected this trend will continue as statistics are beginning to come out in support of employer-approved setups reflected in the estimate that 56 percent of the US workforce holds a job that is compatible (at least partially) with remote work.[2]

2. **Providing Social Connectivity**—Teams thrive on social connection from working together, learning together, and playing together, and although good leaders understand this, great leaders find ways to stay connected in a crisis. Outreach programs are the cornerstone for ensuring those in need are met where they live to get the help they need to return to the life they deserve.

   The need for fellowship, collaboration, and social interaction has become evidenced by the separation and isolation so many of our teams have experienced in the wake of the pandemic. Although the stay-at-home provisions are linked to the virus in 2020, the outcomes and plans put in place to join our teams on social platforms designed to bring us back together will serve us well in a future crisis where distancing or lack of ability to come together persists.

   Creating dedicated spaces for employees to socialize is necessary for teams to stay emotionally connected and healthy. This replaces the actual water cooler and break room with a group of faces in squares we need to see not just hear. The real value resides in their ability to talk about what is on their mind from sharing discoveries related to improving the work-from-home experience to sharing family updates through photos and funny stories, or workout tips.

   These and other topics like recipes including a new version on banana bread are needed in boosting their moods and restore connections they need to the teams they belong to. In turn, this provides more focused members for the critical work that needs to continue and come at it refreshed, engaged, and productive. Virtual coffee breaks or a PD day of yoga, mental health exercises or how to maximize technology, provide more than actual knowledge, tips, and skill; they keep us together and allow for teams to do what they do best—share, care, and grow.

3. **Training for Online Collaboration**—Planning once again determines the level of success teams will experience with online collaboration. Those that trained prior to the first wave of closures and "stay-at-home" orders had the confidence, equipment, and knowledge to accomplish the

work and effectuate the mission from their remote locations. Those who failed to plan—failed to produce the needed activities or were simply left without the ability to work and therefore furloughed or let go.

Developing the agility to pivot based on changes in market conditions must include changes in our ability to travel and connect to others in order to complete basic transactions and complex tasks that are vital to every organization such as processing payroll, payment of taxes, and payment of bills.

In the effort to curb the spread of the virus, shutdowns continue to bring chaos to lives and economies around the world. But efforts to plan and train teams to work together and stay connected remotely through online collaboration will bolster and strengthen those teams until they are rejoined.

4. **Fostering Positive Coping Mechanisms**—As a mentor I often counsel and advise colleagues and junior managers with these words that are fitting and apt for this consideration:

> Situations happen, they often have nothing to do with us—we didn't cause them and we are not responsible for the fact that they happened. What we are responsible for and what we are judged by is how we respond to them—What we do or fail to do in the aftermath of the crisis is what matters.

Driving care initiatives for our team members provide them with coping strategies that foster resilience during a crisis. This goes beyond benefiting the member or their families; it benefits the team as a whole since we are strongest when each member is at their best.

Team performance centers around the quality of the team, area of expertise, skill level, and an understanding of how the team functions during specific threats or challenges. A strong value is placed on the well-being of each member of the team in order to ensure that member is operationally ready at all times. Teams that enjoy a high state of readiness are teams that are capable of answering the call whenever it comes and whatever it takes. That is what makes them invaluable to the organizations they serve. If a member is in crisis, the team is affected.

So on a larger scale, how do we accomplish this? How do we continuously come up with strategies and initiative that deliver the needed boost to ignite our teams and prepare them for the challenges to come? We start by truly caring for them and their circumstance.

Employee Assistant Programs (EAPs) were designed to do just that. An EAP is a great resource to provide outside help that is specialized in delivering care and assistance to those we care about (our team members) in ways that allow them to maintain focus on our needs as a company or organization. It keeps them performing at a level that is beneficial to the teams they support or lead knowing that their personal circumstance is under control or being dealt with thanks to the organization they serve.

Not sure where to start? Or need to get a quick comparison of your current provider? Just search by going online. Shortlister, an online vendor database and sourcing company that helps companies select vendors in the wellness, HR technology and benefits space provides a list of over forty EAP providers with a focus on the Top 12 EAP Providers—Q4 as of October 2020.[3]

I recently spoke at a company in South Jersey who was looking to find ways to keep their team engaged and give them a little boost during the pandemic that put a halt on many company activities designed to recognize and reward them and their families.

AllRisk Property Damage Experts, Inc., located in Runnemede, New Jersey, is a company dedicated to team building and recognizes their teams as the driving force behind their twenty-five-year success. The owner and principal, Frank N. Messina, is a larger than life presence who exudes pride, caring, and determination for his company and its lifeblood—his team.

The son of Italian immigrants, Frank took the lessons learned in the tough family-connected community of South Philadelphia and teamed up with Dean Ragone in 1988 to build what would become AllRisk, Inc. Together with cofounder and current partner Ziggy Osinski, chief operating officer and SVP of construction, they manage a small business employing over seventy people, generating more than $23 million in annual sales with a company profile found on Dun and Bradstreet and Bloomberg.

The two frontmen for the group are women, each smart and talented, with enthusiasm about the core values of the company and how the team they represent allows them to make promises they know will be kept when the time comes to deliver on those promises. Christine Messina, senior vice president of sales and marketing, and Lisa Ortiz, client relations manager, are at the heart of connecting clients. By providing them with solutions to mitigate risk and recover from natural disasters by supplying help in the form of certified and motivated specialists to remove debris, clean up and rebuild and restore physical plants and offices to pre-damaged levels.

What grabbed my attention was the way they have implemented their business model to center on the team approach. From the full-length mural of team members in the conference room to the creative atmosphere, color scheme, and logo that permeates the organization from the jackets and hats they wear to the vans they drive, they are part of a team. Best of all, they are engaged and want to be there.

Although they remained "socially distanced" during the presentation, they remained connected with management. In place of the customary group meal that would have been shared as part of the event; individual bags of soft pretzels were provided for each team member to grab on the way out, along with a copy of my book, *Avoiding Poor Decisions*.

Again, the takeaway is not that they (AllRisk) put together a professional team-building opportunity for their team members, supervisors, managers, and executives; it is that they did so at a time when social distancing was all but ending any opportunity to bring teams together. Making it special by providing a small gift reinforced their commitment to professional development and care for their teams. The continuous heartfelt thanks was evidenced by the pause as many fought back the urge to give a hug or warm embrace to Christine and Lisa and instead opted for an air hug or fist pumps with smiling eyes amid a sea of masks.

Another concept for boosting team performance is teaming (*pairing two or more things in a coordinated ensemble*)[4] in a way that adds value to the process of idea generation. Teams within teams or sub-teams represent temporary groups that function as a unit to accomplish individual goals within the larger set of goals for the organization.

This notion gives rise to the concept of "teaming with meaning" or defined purpose. It draws from the idea of enhancement—providing an improvement, intensification, or magnification of the individual strengths possessed by team members to improve and generate better outcomes. This is how we *maximize human resources* by ensuring we are capitalizing on individual skills, knowledge, and creativity, and in turn allowing them to benefit from the strengths of others in achieving common goals and enjoying combined success. By seizing on our diversity, we provide access to unique skills that individuals in the group possess and strengthen the group by sharing them; however, when we team individuals with the same strengths, we get the power of those strengths multiplied.

In the study of mathematics, *"power"* is defined as *"the number of times as indicated by an exponent that a number occurs as a factor in a product."*[5] In business, we gain better outcomes by achieving higher productivity, thus increasing the strength of our team by combining the strengths of individual members of those teams. Therefore, once teaming is adopted, we are using multiplication of strength to achieve a larger impact, thus yielding a larger product. That's power!

When it comes to idea generation and innovation, our explorations will produce better results when we combine the talents and skills of our team members (*strengths*) as often as possible and feasible through teaming. This approach is what leads great teams to discovery and newfound efficiencies in their practices and procedures. "Why should managers care about teaming? The answer is simple. Teaming is the engine of organizational learning."[6]

Teaming is an action driven by the pursuit of improvement whether that pursuit is "Improvement of instruction" in education, "Increasing productivity" in manufacturing or "Increasing knowledge and research" that leads to breakthroughs in medicine. The bottom line is it's a fluid process that is adaptive to the changing needs we encounter in our environments, regardless of our field of study or line of work. How does it happen? When should it be applied? How do we embed this concept into our practices when teams are already in place throughout our organizations? The answer is quite simple and rooted in the use of the word "teaming" as a *verb* versus a *noun*:

> Teaming is a verb. It is a dynamic activity, not a bounded, static entity. It is largely determined by the mindset and practices of teamwork, not by the design and structures of effective teams. Teaming is teamwork on the fly. It involves coordinating and collaborating without the benefit of stable team structures, because many operations like hospitals, power plants, and military installations require a level of staffing flexibility that makes stable team composition rare. In a growing number of organizations, the constantly shifting nature of work means that many teams disband almost as soon as they've formed. You could be working on one team right now, but in a few days, or even a few minutes, you may be on another team.[7]

This defined usage of teaming as a verb only serves to answer the questions of *who*, *what*, and *why*. At the same time, it ignores the *when*, *where*, or *how* in applying and achieving teaming.

For this, we move to the work of Bruce Tuckman. Tuckman, an American psychological researcher who in 1965 published a theory known as "Tuckman's Stages of Group Development," captured the *when, where,* and *how* through the following designation of four distinct stages: *Forming—Storming—Norming—Performing.* In 1973 the work was expanded to add a final stage: *Adjourning* (figure 8.1).

In the first stage, **Forming**, we often find groups being put together into small teams on an ad-hoc basis for a particular purpose. While the overall practice yields desirable and effective results, this stage can be awkward for some as they are not sure of what to expect from other members of the group, and yet others will find it exciting to team with new people and begin a new challenge. Either way, the groups are formed and they begin the process of learning about the opportunities and challenges they are met with as they start to formulate agreed upon goals, then commence to addressing tasks. While new groups need to work out issues in this phase that center around self-importance and self-concern, leaders within those groups tend to facilitate the process and model appropriate behavior. Once the team has outlined the scope of work related to each task, the group continues to move toward the next phase of group development, **Storming**.

In this phase, **Storming**, we see power struggles, differences of opinion, debate, and strong arguments for what individuals or members of the group

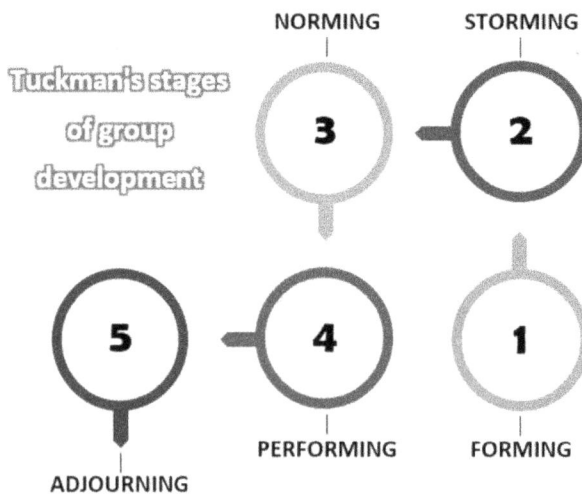

Figure 8.1 Tuckman's Stages of Group Development. *Source:* Self–created.

perceive as the best way to attack a task or accomplish the goal(s). In certain instances, differences and confusion arise over goals, roles, and approaches instead of working together for the greater good. This is especially true of groups forced together who do not know each other prior to the grouping. So what should we do as supervisors?—Nothing! Let them work it out as long as they continue to make progress and as such move forward in the process.

> Storming can be a painful but productive time for a team. A leader's role is not to step in like a parent every time their kids fight but to closely monitor the immerging conflicts with the anticipation they will work themselves out in a productive manner. Increased individual and group pride, confidence and respect are often the result of productive storming. Only step in if the conflict is becoming unproductive and destructive to the team or individual.[8]

A classic case of this is a jury. Typically, twelve individuals who are put together based on a random selection for duty and put through questioning by both attorneys for agreement to join a group whose task is to find the defendant(s) guilty or innocent. If you've ever been on a jury, you would agree the group goes through the very same steps to get to the end result of delivering a verdict. While it may get ugly, they always find a way to get the job done or at least come to a civilized decision even if they return a non-verdict.

While passionate and sometimes even testy, individuals in the group can become easily irritated, impatient, and somewhat bad-tempered while the group works out the issues and reconciles their differences in order to find consensus and an agreed upon plan of attack while moving into the next phase or stage of the development, *Norming*.

In the *Norming* stage groups take on a sense of confidence as they gain momentum in completing the task(s) assigned. Groups develop agreements on the approach and begin seeing themselves as a team working to achieve common goals. Relationships are formed as members begin to relate to one another and see their effort(s) as a shared responsibility. A spirit of cooperation permeates the group, and differences are accepted and no longer seen as roadblocks to accomplishing the goal(s) as distrust and suspicion are replaced with acceptance and tolerance.

Performing is achieved when the group really hits its stride, group norms have been established and roles. This is where the focus on achieving common goals becomes a reality and groups produce the desired outcomes often exceeding the leaders who grouped them. Strong groups become evidenced by their autonomy, enhanced knowledge, shared competencies, and high degree of motivation. These characteristics allow them to gain satisfaction, be rewarded, and enjoy success.

Adjourning—Once the group has achieved success, it will be dissolved and individuals go back to their normal duties and regular places on the larger team(s) depending on the organization. The exercise allows groups to learn how to work together in a collaborative effort for a particular purpose or campaign. As teams utilize this approach to specific tasks, they become more familiar with the process and shorten the storming phase.

Chapter 9

Unleashing Potential

Leveling up today is synonymous with video games and has found its way into our vernacular of employee management and productivity. In the video gaming world, it has taken on an expectation with a multitude of top games built around the concept—to keep players engaged and committed to the game as they work to improve their skills, acquire points or upgrades, and ultimately level up to the next challenge.

By embracing this concept and integrating it into our strategies, we move our "players"—our employees—to the next level thus unleashing their full potential.

Unshackling potential allows for personal motivation to thrive in an environment of possibilities.

The purpose of team building is to develop the strength of our group(s) to achieve larger lifts and secure greater victories with an army of dedicated individuals who share in a belief of team, company, and goals. Our responsibility as leaders is to lead our teams in a way that fosters self-reliance, self-assuredness, trust, and commitment from within each member and for each member of the team in a way that put the team's needs ahead of individual's needs. It is not about any one individual; it is about the team and what the team needs to accomplish in order to provide for all members of the team and the organization. That is how teams need to think, that is how teams need to work together, and that is how teams will be successful.

When contemplating ways to accomplish this, I spent considerable time over the years talking with other leaders, team members, and high achievers that exhibit the characteristics we as managers look for in attracting, hiring, and retaining talent. As a result of those conversations and observations, I put together ten ways to unleash real potential in this infographic and will break it down over the rest of this chapter (figure 9.1).

Clarity of Purpose—By setting realistic goals and expectations for our teams, we ensure a basis of understanding for each member of those teams. This is achieved through continuous communication throughout the organization from directors to managers and team leaders, typically supervisors and department managers who provides guidance, instruction, direction, and leadership.

Ten Ways to Unleash Real Potential

Clarity of Purpose
Setting realistic goals & expectations for the team and individuals

01

02
Collegial Atmosphere
Developing a positive and collaborative culture

Recognition & Rewards Program
Focused on achievement, performance and appreciation

03

04
Professional Settings
Focused on providing spaces and elements that are creative, supportive and inspiring

Climate of Trust
High trust environment with mutual respect, honesty, and open communication

05

06
Honest Feedback
Positive Reinforcement through advice, coaching and counsel

Autonomy
Inspired through a sense of self-worth and self-respect to take actions independently

07

08
Humanize Your Team Building
Personalizing our approach in dealing with teams through care, compassion and concern

Keep Them Informed
Establishment of team meetings, briefings, progress reports and shared outcomes

09

10
Confidence in Risk Taking
Fostering innovation and input into process development with the freedom to fail

Figure 9.1   **Ten Ways to Unleash Real Potential.** *Source*: Self-created.

This is only made possible when those leaders are connected to the mission with enough detail and knowledge regarding the big picture—the *"why."*

Clarity of purpose unites behaviors and actions inside an organization to deliver meaningful experiences.[1]

Clarity of purpose allows each member of the organization to start their day with reason and focus based on a set of goals and objectives that guide their work, their interactions with other team members, customers, and clients and individuals they report to in the organization. When we know what is expected from us, we have the opportunity to deliver; when we are talented, we are capable of exceeding those expectations, and as Fat Amy would say, "Crushing It."

Leading with clarity frees up resources as time, supplies, and materials are dedicated to pathways of success and not wasted following dead ends. Today we speak of "superstars" or "rock stars" when referring to those on teams who stand out as real achievers, leaders, and self-motivated doers.

Unleashing potential means guiding their efforts through purpose. Providing opportunities to operationalize the vision of the company or organization and allowing those rock stars (top performers) to perform or strut their stuff, write their music (creative design), and produce their songs (develop process), we unleash the desire from the passion within.

When we are passionate, we care—it's that simple.

When we care, we do better no matter what it is we chose to do. In turn, we need to instill the same degree of care in our people by providing reason in their efforts.

1. **Collegial Atmosphere**—Developing a positive and collaborative culture allows individuals and teams to thrive and accomplish unmeasurable success in ways that are unthought-of due to excitement, creativity, and synergy. When teams are allowed to create, they unleash their passion, drive, and enthusiasm for invention by redefining the standards to go above and beyond what is known. This places them in the category of explorers, and as such, they adopt a sense of limitless expectations and outcomes.

As leaders, we need to figure out how to move our people forward. To do this, we need to understand them—how they think, how they work, what motivates them, and what they are missing or lacking to become better and more productive. Before we can help others level up, we need to understand what level they are on and what they need in order to move up—resources, opportunity, inspiration, and confidence.

It starts by meeting people where they are and getting them to see where they can go—how they can attain more through a collaborative and collegial atmosphere that nurtures growth and leads to discovery, achievement, and attainment.

> Collaborative leadership includes the purposeful actions we take as leaders to enhance . . . deep relationships with all stakeholders, and deepen our learning together. It includes the managerial side, as well as instructional and transformational leadership, and is the greater whole of all of those parts.[2]

Working in a collegial environment demands collaboration and face it; when people collaborate, they share in the responsibility of the group that includes ensuring individual needs are met and coaching becomes the norm to ensure the success of everyone.

2. **Recognition and Rewards Programs**—Focused on achievement, performance, and appreciation, rewards programs allow us to celebrate the accomplishment, reward the effort, and convey respect for individuals that give of themselves for our success. Individuals that go beyond what is expected truly deserve recognition, appreciation, and celebration.

    In the military, awards ceremonies are sacred. When your name is called, and you break ranks, it starts an immediate rush of adrenaline and pride as you come out in front of your squad, platoon, company, or brigade to receive a medal. Being honored for your dedication and service, hearing those esteemed words of, "In keeping with the finest traditions . . . bringing credit upon yourself, your unit and the Branch," is like nothing else. Trust me; it's a big deal!

    Recognition and rewards programs are easy and inexpensive. They require time and attention-to-detail to plan and execute. To ensure they have meaning, they must be authentic.

    Fifteen years ago, I started an annual kick-off meeting for the custodial/maintenance team that included breakfast (eggs, bacon, waffles, and extras) to make it more than just muffins and coffee. It gives them time to eat together and visit, build relationships with team members from other schools in the district and allows us to thank the men and women who give their time and effort throughout the year to ensure our buildings are cared for and our classrooms are ready.

I added a featured speaker each year to give them professional development beyond their daily tasks, centered on leadership. Having speakers allowed me an opportunity as a speaker and presenter to open with a customized presentation on a different theme each year that tied to our district goals and initiatives.

The featured speaker or keynote was always some professional with linkage to what they (the custodial/maintenance team) had a hand in based on their work or upcoming special projects that year.

For example, our risk manager from Willis Towers Watson, a global company with over 45,000 employees and interests in more than 140 countries and markets, provided risk management tips for the group. By selecting the speakers, based on the relationship to custodial/maintenance operations, it gave us a strategic advantage by showing them the big picture and how essential their part is in achieving it.

By elevating the importance and self-worth of individuals, we get them to try harder, deliver better results, and exhibit more care. Improved performance is the result of realized value. By having value, we become important, important to the team and organization as a whole.

Everyone wants to be important—everyone wants to matter. It is inherent in our makeup to be important and valued as individuals with something to contribute and share.

Finally, they needed an audience to bear witness to the ceremony beyond their leaders, so we made it larger in importance by inviting select guests, supervisors, directors, principals, our superintendent, and members of the Board of Education. Equally important, we asked our guests to arrive early for the breakfast so they could mingle and get to know our staff.

Just like board meetings, we asked the board president and superintendent to come up to the podium once we started the awards ceremony to heighten the importance of the awards. Having them hand out each award to individuals as their name is called increases the prestige of the event. In addition, we had the communications officer on hand to take photos and prepare short write-ups for our website, social media, and local press.

To ensure awards are meaningful and real, we limit the offering based on real achievement versus participation or group awards.

Awards should be earned and only given to those who are deserving of them; handing them out like "Pez" diminishes their value and downgrades their worth.

Our awards range from certificates of appreciation signed by the superintendent of schools to top honors each year for a select few who earn the prestigious and coveted Leadership Award, signed by the board president. The Leadership Award comes framed along with a gift certificate.

Each year the event gets better, and we started having neighboring district administrators as visitors based on our success and word of the program. In total, the event costs us about six hours of prep time and somewhere around $200 for awards and $400 for the breakfast. We successfully get our guest company to sponsor the event and cover the cost of breakfast; so for $200 we provide a low-cost high-impact event for this special team of individuals.

4. **Professional Settings**—Workplaces that are centered on optimal space utilization, designed to accommodate ergonomic needs, and are aesthetically pleasing work to inspire, motivate, and allow for a sense of pride and ownership. Pride in where you work begins with the setup in which you are expected to work your magic. Who doesn't want the corner office or any office with a view? Reality is there are only so many windows in any office set up, so this is unrealistic.

   In large organizations many individuals do not even have an office, and find themselves clustered with other team members in a busy, chaotic environment where they all share the copier, trade off answering the phone or buzzing the door and tuning each other out as they focus on their work or their phone call.

   While space dictates the limits of our floor plans, imagination, thought, and design can improve and expand those spaces in order to unleash the creativity within our teams. Upgrades like standing desks, flooring, and decorative elements and furniture suited to ergonomic needs make a big difference. Color schemes can brighten, inspire, and warm spaces to allow working together to take on new meaning and increase productivity.

   The environment where people work has a direct effect on their productivity as well as creativity. So, it becomes imperative to give serious thought to the workspace design.[3]

Taking steps to reimagine the workplace by creating "genius centers," a new design to engage students, and enhance learning through collaborative settings can be pushed up to adults in how we arrange conference rooms, action labs, and meeting rooms.

By *"busting out* and *busting up"* walls and ceilings to add daylighting and brighten the mood by unleashing imagination, creativity, and discovery. Adding color and personalizing the workspace to reflect the positive mood and sense of belonging while providing opportunity to stand out with personal style, flair, and interest is what needs to carry the day in office space design.

Get inspired with vibrant colors and themes that electrify the spaces your teams inhabit for hours on end, avoiding the trapped sense of prison or "institutional blue" that faded hue that sends vibes of depression, hopelessness, and nothing.

"A recent University of Texas study found that bland gray, beige and white offices induced feelings of sadness and depression, especially in women. Men, on the other hand, experienced similarly gloomy feelings in purple and orange workspaces."[4] Studies have shown colors can actually impact productivity levels;[5] the choice in color will determine whether that impact is positive or negative. The takeaway—research before you paint.

5. **Climate of Trust**—High-trust environments are those with mutual respect, honesty, and open communications. They produce better and faster results in keeping with the concept, "Speed of Trust,"[6] expressed by Stephen Covey. Covey covers this concept in his third wave of trust, under the umbrella of Organizational Trust.

   As simple as it sounds when organizations exercise trust, they *straighten up and fly right*; it's a realignment of the competencies of their teams with the goals of the organization in support of the mission by supporting each other. The third wave, organizational trust, centers around alignment.

   When low trust pervades an organization, people manipulate facts, withhold information, and resist new ideas or positive change. They cover up or cover over mistakes and mislead or outright lie to one another or management.

   Likewise, managers are slow to pass honest or vital information to peers in fear of falling behind or giving them a tactical advantage, and they are famous for keeping subordinates in the dark regarding processes or why actions are being taken. As a result, the day-to-day activities suffer and the work produced pales in comparison to output and outcomes of high-trust organizations.

When we operate in a climate of high trust, people open up, and once unguarded they are left brimming with excitement, possibilities, and desire to produce results.

6. **Honest Feedback**—Positive Reinforcement through advice, coaching and counsel is proven to be the most effective way to lead. Not only is it effective, it is much easier and considerably more enjoyable as people prefer good news over bad.

   In a 2020 Zenger Folkman Feedback Management Study,[7] this statement is proven to be accurate and effective based on data taken from 360-degree assessments of leaders regarding their effectiveness rating. In the global survey of more than 12,600 leaders, they asked what their preference was for giving negative or positive feedback. Of the group surveyed, 62 percent reported a preference of giving negative feedback and 36 percent reported that they avoided giving people positive feedback. The basic assumption is that negative feedback allows for greater improvement as individuals can focus on their weaknesses.

   Zenger and Folkman took a subset or segment of the group and obtained 360-degree assessment data to graph the leaders on an effectiveness scale based on their ability to give honest feedback in a helpful way.

   The breakthrough discovery came after the findings revealed *leaders with a propensity to give positive feedback scored higher than their counterparts who avoided giving positive feedback* or feedback of any kind.

   Leaders fell into two distinct categories; those who gave positive feedback and avoided negative feedback (group C) and those who gave both positive and negative feedback (group D) scored higher, both in the fifty-first percentile for effective leadership (figure 9.2).

The most negatively rated group were those leaders who said they avoided giving positive feedback and preferred to give negative feedback (Group B).

The clear takeaway from the research proven by Zenger and Folkman regarding the effects of positive feedback and higher effectiveness ratings for leaders is that both groups who scored in the fifty-first percentile on effectiveness included *positive feedback*.

Effectiveness Ranking of Leaders by Reports
ZENGER|FOLKMAN 2020

GROUP A	GROUP B	GROUP C	GROUP D
44%	**39%**	**51%**	**51%**
No Feedback	Avoid + only -	Gives + Avoid -	Gives Both
84 Respondents	333 Respondents	192 Respondents	396 Responents

Figure 9.2   Zenger-Folkman 2020 Survey on Effectiveness of Positive Feedback. *Source:* Self-created.

At the same time those who gave *negative feedback* and *positive feedback* contained the largest number of respondents, 396 (Group D) and accounted for the largest percentage of the sub-group or 39.4 percent compared with the second largest group (Group B) at 33.1 percent representing the lowest effectiveness rating, only reaching the thirty-ninth percentile.

So while positive feedback is encouraged, honest feedback includes discussion on both strengths and weaknesses in a positive way that encourages growth and instills confidence in one's ability to increase performance. Keep it focused, keep it positive, and keep it honest. Avoiding telling people what they are doing well or doing great is just as bad as telling some they are good when they are not—both are dishonest.

7. **Autonomy**—Inspired through a sense of self-worth and self-respect; autonomy provides latitude for teams in decision making that unleashes personal motivation. When teams are given authority to take action based on clear guidance, direction, and an understanding of the situation at hand, things get done right. When we trust others to do their jobs, we benefit by drawing from a reservoir of motivation, creativity, and passion.

   The opposite is micro-managing, a constant state of overbearing questioning, or a debilitating structure of approval prior to any action being taken, that not only slows production or progress; it dampens spirit, drive, and enthusiasm.

Anyone who has worked with me understands this well as I express my attitude regarding autonomy as such, "If I have to do your job, then I don't need you." I trust people can generally do their job and given the tools, trust and confidence will perform well.

Autonomy allows teams to do what they were hired and trained to do and become better at it as they take on more responsibility. And just to be clear, *as leaders we can delegate authority but never responsibility*, so we remain responsible for the work product and actions of our teams. When they fail, we fail; however, a failed attempt is simply a progression in the search for success so have patience.

8. **Humanize Your Team Building**—Personalizing our approach in dealing with teams through care, compassion, and concern is free and easy—start by remembering they are people. While it is easy to get wrapped up in getting work done, sometimes we lose sight of that fact and are quick to anger or frustration when the heat is on, the pressure is mounting, and someone drops the ball—yelling and screaming at them won't help them get it together.

   Instead of losing your cool, learn to stay calm. Staying calm is a learned trait that separates great leaders from those who are just in-charge. When you are calm, those in your charge are calmer even in high-stress situations. They feed off your energy and they are already on edge because they know things aren't going as well as expected or true to plan. When you are calm, they can relax enough to regroup and rework the problem or adjust their course, take a different approach, or start over. A sense of calm in dealing with individuals in a productive way to address any issue will result in a better outcome. Stress and anger short circuit our ability to think and therefore produce, solve, or create.

   Take a deep breath, and instead of anger or frustration, try adopting a laser focus to the issue at hand and work with the individual to get them and the team back on track. This is how great leaders keep their teams focused and keep those teams *busting out the work* that needs to happen while *problem-solving* the setbacks and *adjusting* to the challenges they encounter.

   Another tip to humanizing your team building is the way you communicate when things are going normal, during routine work and periods of low stress.

Try writing a personal note or card for a birthday or other occasion. Thank you cards are still highly valued and thoughtful ways to express care.

Whenever someone takes the time to handwrite a card, note, or message, it deepens the connection and adds a human touch that people appreciate and remember. For millennials, however, an upbeat text may be just the thing to do the job, and that's even faster. The difference is in knowing your team and what they would respond best to in accomplishing this.

9. **Keep Them Informed**—The establishment of team meetings, briefings, and progress reports is a good way to ensure those on the team are connected and involved in the generation of successful outcomes. We've all heard the phrase, "The left-hand doesn't know what the right hand is doing"; sadly it is still alive and well in dysfunctional operations with poorly run teams.

   When a team member does not understand the mission or what others on the team are doing or why, they run into serious problems when someone on the team goes down, calls out, or takes an unexpected leave. Even when everyone is present, they are not a cohesive unit. Instead of functioning as one unit, they are disjointed, doing individual tasks with no adjustment, concern, or modifications for others who may need a piece of what they are doing to help finish their job.

   Keeping teams informed allows them to be responsive to the needs of the organization, which causes them to work in harmony, with purpose and importance.

10. **Confidence in Risk-Taking**—Fostering innovation and input into process development with the freedom to fail is what leads to discovery. "Risk takers are more likely to be successful because they do not limit themselves and are willing to put in their energy when every other person is hesitant."[8]

    By allowing our teams to take risks, we are permitting them to think bigger, take chances, and become passionate about what we do and how we can do it better. Ideas thrive in an open environment that rewards risk-takers. Some of the greatest inventions have come at the expense of risk-taking.

    I walked into a PD opportunity a year ago that inspired the first chapter of the book *Problem-Solving Today, The Importance of Problem Solving*

Skills (Beyond I.Q.). A group of principals and supervisors had placed five items on tables for each group, along with a pad to record our ideas for an invention we would have to market to the larger group.

The items placed on the table are what intrigued the group as we were all asked to find the common denominator. Those items were Playdough, Post-It notes, a Slinky, Silly Putty, and a bag of potato chips. What was it about these items that pulled them together into the same family? Was it that they were all manufactured by the same company? No. Could it be that they were all items found in the dollar store? Maybe, but that wasn't what they were looking for—so keep thinking. Where they all made from plastic? Luckily the answer to that question and was No.

So why the game? What was it about these items that tied to professional development and learning?

It was that they came into being as mistakes made by scientists in search of other discoveries. And that risk-taking was not only ok; it was encouraged in our organization. Consider the elements above in the first nine points to unleash potential that gave these leaders access, opportunity, and confidence to present on risk-taking to other leaders in the organization including their bosses.

The message they were sending was, it's better to try and fail than not try at all—but the try's or attempts produce learning and knowledge. And sometimes we discover new things or ways to do something that have significant benefits for all. The whole premise behind "Risk-Reward" is taking chances often results in success! Mission accomplished—We have a winner!

Epilogue/Conclusion

Teams increase both our *capability* to deal with issues and our *capacity* to handle multiple issues simultaneously. As demonstrated throughout this book, *the strength of the team* is the driving factor behind success in organizations, athletics, and business.

Recently, I binge-watched the top-rated series *The Queen's Gambit* on Netflix, which delivered nothing short of the promised captivation, intrigue, and sexiness centered around the 1960s and the game of chess. What a combination!

What grabbed at my intellect, besides the fact that I will never be even close to playing at that level, was the focus on the *importance of the team* on an individual sport, shown to be the chief factor in giving the Russian players an edge over their international challengers. That realization of *strength through team* is what pushed the American Phenom Beth Harman (Anya Taylor-Joy) over the top in the final game against Grandmaster Vasily Vorgov (Marcin Dorocinski) in the final episode, "End Game."

I find it interesting that although the storyline is based on true games of the time tied to Bobby Fischer and Anatoly Karpov, the writers thought if it's worthy to point out the need to incorporate the use of teams in training, preparation, and improvement of play for the individual. Coaching and team strategizing by exploring every possible combination on the board by her loyal group of peers gave Harman her footing at a crucial point in the game the same way mentors and teammates help us succeed at decisive moments in our careers. Teams are what allow us to rise above those challenges to gain our victories.

Notes

CHAPTER 1

1. Roth, John. "What Gladiators Can Teach Us About Honor," January 17, 2018. Accessed August 5, 2020. https://goodmenproject.com/featured-content/gladiators-teach-honor-chwm/.

2. Sherman, Richard M. 1928–. *Walt Disney's The Jungle Book*. Milwaukee, WI: Hal Leonard, 1994.

3. *Remember the Titans*. Directed by Boaz Yakin, presented by Walt Disney Pictures in association with Jerry Bruckheimer Films a Technical Black production; a Boaz Yakin film; produced by Jerry Bruckheimer, Chad Oman; written by Gregory Allen Howard. Burbank, CA: Walt Disney Home Video: Distributed by Buena Vista Home Entertainment, 2007.

4. Core, Ericson. 2006. *Invincible*. United States: Buena Vista Pictures.

5. "Walt Disney Company (The) Common Stock (DIS) Financials." Nasdaq. Accessed September 12, 2020. https://www.nasdaq.com/market-activity/stocks/dis/financials.

6. "Disney Net Worth 2006-2020: DIS." Macrotrends. Accessed September 12, 2020. https://www.macrotrends.net/stocks/charts/DIS/disney/net-worth.

7. Jones, Bruce. "Leadership Lessons from Walt Disney: Building Relationships." Disney Institute Blog. Disney, June 12, 2018. Accessed September 13, 2020. https://www.disneyinstitute.com/blog/leadership-lessons-from-walt-disney-building-relationships/.

8. Robertson, Lee. "Why the Sense of Belonging Is Crucial to Teamwork." AoEC Global, July 18, 2020. Accessed September 13, 2020. https://www.aoec.com/knowledge-bank/why-the-sense-of-belonging-is-crucial-to-teamwork/.

9. Schatz, Traci. "What Makes Teamwork Effective?" Small Business - Chron.com. Chron.com, February 4, 2019. Accessed September 13, 2020. https://smallbusiness.chron.com/teamwork-effective-694.html.

10. "Invincible (2006) - Financial Information." The Numbers. Accessed September 12, 2020. https://www.the-numbers.com/movie/Invincible-(2006).

11. "Remember the Titans (2000) - Financial Information." The Numbers. Accessed September 12, 2020. https://www.the-numbers.com/movie/Remember-the -Titans-(2000).

12. Cooke, Nancy J., and Margaret L. Hilton. *Enhancing the Effectiveness of Team Science*. Washington, DC: The National Academies Press, 2015.

13. "5 Teams That Failed to Stay Afloat (And What Sank Them)." CMOE, March 11, 2019. Accessed September 13, 2020. https://cmoe.com/blog/big-teams-that-failed/.

14. Ibid.

15. Ibid.

16. Sauter, Michael B. "The Worst Companies to Work For." 247 Wall St. 24/7 Wall St., January 12, 2020. Accessed September 13, 2020. https://247wallst.com/ special-report/2017/06/05/the-worst-companies-to-work-for-3/4/.

17. Ibid.

18. "The Many (Law)Suits of Forever 21." The Finery Report. The Finery Report, October 2, 2019. Accessed September 13, 2020. https://www.thefineryreport.com/ articles/2019/10/2/the-many-lawsuits-of-forever-21.

19. Wikipedia contributors, "Action Plan," Wikipedia, The Free Encyclopedia. Accessed September 19, 2020. https://en.wikipedia.org/w/index.php?title=Action _plan&oldid=985728940.

20. Wikipedia contributors, "Scientia potentia est," Wikipedia, The Free Encyclopedia. Accessed September 20, 2020. https://en.wikipedia.org/w/index.php?title =Scientia_potentia_est&oldid=967457714.

21. McFarlane, Sam. "Shared Leadership has Benefits for Everyone." Collective Possibilities, July 10, 2014. Adapted from HBR Blog by Marshall Goldsmith. Accessed September 20, 2020. http://www.collectivepossibilities.com.au/whats-new/ shared-leadership-has-benefits-for-everyone/.

22. Ibid.

23. Merriam-Webster.com Dictionary, s.v. "discourse," accessed September 16, 2020, https://www.merriam-webster.com/dictionary/discourse.

24. Martinelli, Katie. "The Importance of Respect in the Workplace: Guide for Managers." The Hub | High Speed Training. High Speed Training, June 10, 2020. Accessed September 21, 2020. https://www.highspeedtraining.co.uk/hub/importance -of-respect-in-the-workplace/.

25. Ibid.

CHAPTER 2

1. O'Dowd, Sean. "Chicago Bulls: Michael Jordan's 10 Best Teammates." Bleacher Report. Bleacher Report, October 3, 2017. Accessed August 16, 2020. https://bleacherreport.com/articles/845166-chicago-bulls-michael-jordans-10-best -teammates.

2. Ibid.

3. *The Last Dance*. Directed by Jason Hehir. Los Gatos, CA: Netflix, ESPN, 2020.

4. Wikipedia contributors, "National Football League Draft," Wikipedia, The Free Encyclopedia. Accessed July 21, 2020. https://en.wikipedia.org/w/index.php ?title=National_Football_League_Draft&oldid=967790555.

5. Murphy, Kristy. "8 Recruitment Strategies to Attract the Best Talent." Blog, April 3, 2020. Accessed August 9, 2020. https://www.talentlyft.com/en/blog/article /211/8-recruitment-strategies-to-attract-the-best-talent.

6. Bika, Nikoletta. "What Is the Average Time to Hire by Industry?" Workable, February 4, 2020. Accessed August 9, 2020. https://resources.workable.com/stories -and-insights/time-to-hire-industry.

7. Ibid.

8. Gagen, Andrew. "Global Recruiting Trends for 2017." LinkedIn. Accessed August 9, 2020. https://www.linkedin.com/pulse/global-recruiting-trends-2017 -andrew-gagen/.

9. Bika, Nikoletta. "What Is the Average Time to Hire by Industry?" Workable, February 4, 2020. Accessed August 9, 2020. https://resources.workable.com/stories -and-insights/time-to-hire-industry.

10. Gentle, Stuart. "The Importance of Social Media in Recruiting." Onrec, September 1, 2017. Accessed August 9, 2020. https://www.onrec.com/news/features/the -importance-of-social-media-in-recruiting.

11. Munasinghe, Kate and Gautier Lalith. "Build a Stronger Employee Referral Program." Harvard Business Review, May 26, 2020. Accessed August 9, 2020. https://hbr.org/2020/05/build-a-stronger-employee-referral-program.

12. Dooley, Roger. "College Branding: The Tipping Point." Forbes. Forbes Magazine, February 5, 2013. Accessed August 11, 2020. https://www.forbes.com/sites/ rogerdooley/2013/02/05/college-branding-tipping/.

13. Ibid.

CHAPTER 3

1. Trull, Samuel G. "Strategies of Effective Interviewing." Harvard Business Review, August 1, 2014. Accessed August 23, 2020. https://hbr.org/1964/01/strategies-of-effective-interviewing.

2. Bikar, Nikoletta. "Structured Interview Questions: Examples and Tips for Hiring: Workable." Recruiting Resources: How to Recruit and Hire Better, September 25, 2020. Accessed September 28, 2020. https://resources.workable.com/tutorial/ structured-interview-questions-guide.

3. "Screening Interviews: Everything You Need to Know." Indeed Career Guide. Accessed October 10, 2020. https://www.indeed.com/career-advice/interviewing/ screening-interview.

CHAPTER 4

1. 2019 Training Industry Report https://trainingmag.com/sites/default/files/2019 _industry_report.pdf.

2. "Why Firing an Employee Is Always the Last Resort." IFP HR Insights for Professionals. January 28, 2019. Accessed October 10, 2020. https://www.insight

sforprofessionals.com/hr/recruitment-and-onboarding/why-firing-employee-last-resort.

3. Stevenson, Mason. "Bad Hiring Costs – By the Numbers." HR Exchange Network. HR Exchange Network, January 10, 2020. Accessed October 10, 2020. https://www.hrexchangenetwork.com/hr-talent-acquisition/articles/poor-hiring-costs-by-the-numbers.

4. Ibid.

5. Ibid.

6. Roberts, Calia. "Reasons for Immediate Termination." Azcentral.com, September 29, 2016. Accessed October 14, 2020. https://yourbusiness.azcentral.com/reasons-immediate-termination-8026.html.

7. Ibid.

8. Wikipedia contributors, "Straighten Up and Fly Right," Wikipedia, The Free Encyclopedia. Accessed October 10, 2020. https://en.wikipedia.org/w/index.php?title=Straighten_Up_and_Fly_Right&oldid=980185876.

9. Jeanne Mejeur, Michelle Larson-Krieg. "At-Will Employment – Overview." NCLS - National Conference of State Legislatures, April 15, 2008. Accessed October 11, 2020. https://www.ncsl.org/research/labor-and-employment/at-will-employment-overview.aspx.

10. Feldman, Frank. "7 Things Employees Get Wrong about 'Wrongful Termination.'" HR Morning, November 1, 2019. Accessed October 11, 2020. https://www.hrmorning.com/articles/wrongful-termination/.

11. Guerin, Lisa, J. D. "What Is Progressive Discipline for Employees?" www.nolo.com. Nolo, January 5, 2012. Accessed October 11, 2020. https://www.nolo.com/legal-encyclopedia/employee-progressive-discipline-basics-30242.html.

12. Knight, Rebecca. "The Right Way to Fire Someone." Harvard Business Review, June 14, 2016. Accessed October 11, 2020. https://hbr.org/2016/02/the-right-way-to-fire-someone.

13. Ibid.

CHAPTER 5

1. Brown, Josh. "The Perfect Employee Evaluation Form: Templates + How-To." Helpjuice, November 27, 2019. Accessed October 21, 2020. https://helpjuice.com/blog/employee-evaluation-form.

2. Merriam-Webster.com Dictionary, s.v. "evaluation." Accessed October 19, 2020. https://www.merriam-webster.com/dictionary/evaluation.

3. "PolicyNL." More Information on the Benefits and Types of Evaluation | Policy NL. Accessed October 20, 2020. https://www.policynl.ca/policydevelopment/pages/information-on-benefits-types-evaluation.html.

4. "What Is The History Of Formative & Summative Evaluations." Tony & Allen, November 16, 2018. Accessed October 20, 2020. http://tony-allen.com/what-is-the-history-of-formative-summative-evaluations/.

CHAPTER 6

1. "Objectives of Performance Appraisal." What is Human Resource? (Defined) Human Resource Management Topics – Labor Laws – High Courts; Supreme Court Citation – Case Laws. Accessed October 23, 2020. http://www.whatishumanresource.com/objectives-of-performance-appraisal.

2. Wholley, Meredith. "17 Mind-Blowing Statistics on Performance Reviews and Employee Engagement." ClearCompany, September 10, 2019. Accessed October 13, 2020. https://blog.clearcompany.com/mind-blowing-statistics-performance-reviews-employee-engagement.

3. "Performance Review Surveys." SurveyMonkey. Accessed October 23, 2020. https://www.surveymonkey.com/mp/performance-review-survey/.

4. Wholley, Meredith. "17 Mind-Blowing Statistics on Performance Reviews and Employee Engagement." ClearCompany, September 10, 2019. Accessed October 13, 2020. https://blog.clearcompany.com/mind-blowing-statistics-performance-reviews-employee-engagement.

5. Corkery, Liz. "Observation & Feedback (Coaching)." Human Resources, October 8, 2019. Accessed October 25, 2020. https://hr.ucdavis.edu/performance-appraisals/supervisor-resources/observation.

6. Fearn, Nicholas, and Brian Turner. "Best Note-Taking Apps for Android in 2020." TechRadar pro. November 28, 2019. Accessed October 23, 2020. https://www.techradar.com/best/best-note-taking-apps-android.

7. "360 Degree Feedback Survey Tool & Questions." SurveyMonkey. Accessed October 27, 2020. https://www.surveymonkey.com/mp/360-employee-feedback-survey-example/.

8. Dweck, Carol. "The Power of Believing That You Can Improve." TED, November 2014. Accessed October 27, 2020. https://www.ted.com/talks/carol_dweck_the_power_of_believing_that_you_can_improve?language=en.

9. Berkowitz, Philip, and James Horton. "Discovery of Personnel Records in Employment Discrimination Cases." New York Law Journal, July 2, 2020. Accessed November 7, 2020. https://www.law.com/newyorklawjournal/2020/07/02/discovery-of-personnel-records-in-employment-discrimination-cases/?slreturn=20200928083810.

10. TRINITY HEALTH CORP and TRINITY HEALTH-MICHIGAN, d/b/a SAINT MARY'S HEALTH CARE (STATE OF MICHIGAN COURT OF APPEALS April 16, 2013).

CHAPTER 7

1. Clark, Dave. "What Do Today''s Employees Really Want from Their Employer?" TTI Success Insights Blog, July 25, 2019. Accessed November 7, 2020. https://blog.ttisi.com/what-do-todays-employees-really-want-from-their-employer.

2. Bureau of Labor Statistics, U.S. Department of Labor, Occupational Outlook Handbook, "The Median Number of Years That Wage and Salary Workers Had Been with Their Current Employer." Accessed November 7, 2020. https://www.bls.gov/opub/ted/2018/median-tenure-with-current-employer-was-4-point-2-years-in-january-2018.htm.

3. Martin, Rob. "Our Methodology." Great Place to Work®. Accessed November 7, 2020. https://www.greatplacetowork.com/our-methodology.

4. Frauenheim, Ed. "Great Place to Work® and Fortune Announce the 2020 World's Best Workplaces™." Great Place to Work®, October 13, 2020. Accessed November 7, 2020. https://www.greatplacetowork.com/press-releases/great-place-to-work-and-fortune-announce-the-2020-world-s-best-workplaces.

5. Freifeld, Lorri. "Dollar General Does It Again." pubs.royle.com. Training Magazine, March/April 2020. Accessed November 14, 2020. https://pubs.royle.com/publication/?i=650103.

6. Ibid.

7. Ibid.

8. "Dollar General: 2020 Fortune 500." Fortune, August 10, 2020. Accessed November 14, 2020. https://fortune.com/company/dollar-general/fortune500/.

9. Dollar General Corporation, 2019 Annual Report (PDF), accessed November 14, 2020, https://investor.dollargeneral.com/download/companies/dollargeneral/Annual%20Reports/AR_2019_Dollar%20General_Web%20PDF.pdf.

10. Ibid.

11. Ibid.

12. Number of stores of Dollar General in the United States from 2007 to 2019. Published by Statista Research, May 28, 2020. Accessed November 14, 2020. https://www.statista.com/statistics/253587/number-of-stores-of-dollar-general-in-the-united-states/.

CHAPTER 8

1. Caligiuri, Paula, and Helen DeCieri. "4 Ways Companies Can Support Their Workers during the Coronavirus Crisis." The Conversation, September 6, 2020. Accessed November 21, 2020. https://theconversation.com/4-ways-companies-can-support-their-workers-during-the-coronavirus-crisis-134732.

2. Lister, Kate. "Work-at-Home After Covid-19-Our Forecast." Global Workplace Analytics, April 12, 2020. Accessed November 22, 2020. https://globalworkplaceanalytics.com/work-at-home-after-covid-19-our-forecast.

3. "List of EAP Providers: Top 11 EAP Companies October 2020." myshortlister.com. Accessed November 22, 2020. https://www.myshortlister.com/eap-providers/vendor-list.

4. Merriam-Webster.com Dictionary, s.v. "team." Accessed October 3, 2020. https://www.merriam-webster.com/dictionary/team.

5. Merriam-Webster.com Dictionary, s.v. "power." Accessed October 4, 2020. https://www.merriam-webster.com/dictionary/power.

6. "The Importance of Teaming." HBS Working Knowledge, April 25, 2012. Accessed October 3, 2020. https://hbswk.hbs.edu/item/the-importance-of-teaming.

7. Ibid.

8. Stratton, Shawn. "5 Tips to Manage the Storming Phase of Group Development." LinkedIn. Accessed October 4, 2020. https://www.linkedin.com/pulse/5-tips -manage-storming-phase-group-development-shawn-stratton.

CHAPTER 9

1. Bliss, Jeanne. "Do You Lead Your Company with Clarity of Purpose?" Customer Bliss. Three Blocks Long, December 9, 2019. Accessed November 24, 2020. https://www.customerbliss.com/lead-with-clarity-of-purpose/.

2. DeWitt, Peter M., John Hattie, and Russell J. Quaglia. *Collaborative Leadership: Six Influences That Matter Most.* Thousand Oaks, CA: Corwin, a SAGE Company, 2017.

3. Somerfield, Claudia. "7 Inspirational Workspace Designs." Work Design Magazine, October 10, 2019. Accessed November 27, 2020. https://www.workdesign .com/2012/02/7-inspirational-workspace-designs/.

4. Lachance-Shandrow, Kim. "How the Color of Your Office Impacts Productivity (Infographic)." Entrepreneur, March 9, 2015. Accessed, November 27, 2020. https://www.entrepreneur.com/article/243749.

5. Steele, Jeffrey. "How Color Psychology Impacts Today's Workplace." Forbes. Forbes Magazine, January 7, 2020. Accessed, November 27, 2020. https://www .forbes.com/sites/jeffsteele/2020/01/06/how-color-psychology-impacts-todays-workplace/?sh=6d5fb01d10b1.

6. Covey, Stephen M. R. *The Speed of Trust.* New York, NY: Free Press, 2006.

7. Folkman, Joseph. "3 Old Assumptions That Haunt Feedback and Halt Progress." ZENGER FOLKMAN, November 3, 2020. Accessed November 29, 2020. https://zengerfolkman.com/articles/3-old-assumptions-that-haunt-feedback-and-halt -progress/.

8. Imafidon, Casey. "8 Reasons Risk Takers Are More Likely To Be Successful." Landit, September 28, 2019. Accessed November 29, 2020. https://landit.com/articles /8-reasons-risk-takers-are-more-likely-to-be-successful.

References

Berkowitz, Philip, and James Horton. "Discovery of Personnel Records in Employment Discrimination Cases." New York Law Journal, July 2, 2020. Accessed November 7, 2020. https://www.law.com/newyorklawjournal/2020/07/02/discovery-of-personnel-records-in-employment-discrimination-cases/?slreturn=20200928083810.

Bika, Nikoletta. "What Is the Average Time to Hire by Industry?" Workable. February 4, 2020. Accessed August 9, 2020. https://resources.workable.com/stories-and-insights/time-to-hire-industry.

Bikar, Nikoletta. "Structured Interview Questions: Examples and Tips for Hiring: Workable." Recruiting Resources: How to Recruit and Hire Better, September 25, 2020. Accessed September 28, 2020. https://resources.workable.com/tutorial/structured-interview-questions-guide.

Bliss, Jeanne. "Do You Lead Your Company with Clarity of Purpose?" Customer Bliss. Three Blocks Long, December 9, 2019. Accessed November 24, 2020. https://www.customerbliss.com/lead-with-clarity-of-purpose/.

Brown, Josh. "The Perfect Employee Evaluation Form: Templates + How-To." Helpjuice, November 27, 2019. Accessed October 21, 2020. https://helpjuice.com/blog/employee-evaluation-form.

Caligiuri, Paula, and Helen DeCieri. "4 Ways Companies Can Support Their Workers during the Coronavirus Crisis." The Conversation, September 6, 2020. Accessed November 21, 2020. https://theconversation.com/4-ways-companies-can-support-their-workers-during-the-coronavirus-crisis-134732.

Clark, Dave. "What Do Today's Employees Really Want from Their Employer?" TTI Success Insights Blog. July 25, 2019. Accessed November 7, 2020. https://blog.ttisi.com/what-do-todays-employees-really-want-from-their-employer.

Cooke, Nancy J., and Margaret L. Hilton. *Enhancing the Effectiveness of Team Science*. Washington, DC: The National Academies Press, 2015.

Core, Ericson. 2006. *Invincible*. United States: Buena Vista Pictures, Burbank, California .

Corkery, Liz. "Observation & Feedback (Coaching)." Human Resources, October 8, 2019. Accessed October 25, 2020. https://hr.ucdavis.edu/performance-appraisals/supervisor-resources/observation.

Covey, Stephen M. R. *The Speed of Trust*. New York, NY: Free Press, 2006.

DeWitt, Peter M., John Hattie, and Russell J. Quaglia. *Collaborative Leadership: Six Influences That Matter Most*. Thousand Oaks, CA: Corwin, a SAGE Company, 2017.

Dooley, Roger. "College Branding: The Tipping Point." Forbes. Forbes Magazine, February 5, 2013. Accessed August 11, 2020. https://www.forbes.com/sites/roger-dooley/2013/02/05/college-branding-tipping/.

Dweck, Carol. "The Power of Believing That You Can Improve." TED. November 2014. Accessed October 27, 2020. https://www.ted.com/talks/carol_dweck_the_power_of_believing_that_you_can_improve?language=en.

Fearn, Nicholas, and Brian Turner. "Best Note-Taking Apps for Android in 2020." TechRadar pro. November 28, 2019. Accessed October 23, 2020. https://www.techradar.com/best/best-note-taking-apps-android.

Feldman, Frank. "7 Things Employees Get Wrong about 'Wrongful Termination'." HR Morning. November 1, 2019. Accessed October 11, 2020. https://www.hrmorning.com/articles/wrongful-termination/.

Folkman, Joseph. "3 Old Assumptions That Haunt Feedback and Halt Progress." ZENGER FOLKMAN, November 3, 2020. Accessed November 29, 2020. https://zengerfolkman.com/articles/3-old-assumptions-that-haunt-feedback-and-halt-progress/.

Frauenheim, Ed. "Great Place to Work® and Fortune Announce the 2020 World's Best Workplaces™." Great Place to Work®, October 13, 2020. Accessed November 7, 2020. https://www.greatplacetowork.com/press-releases/great-place-to-work-and-fortune-announce-the-2020-world-s-best-workplaces.

Freifeld, Lorri. "Dollar General Does It Again." pubs.royle.com. Training Magazine, March/April 2020. Accessed November 14, 2020. https://pubs.royle.com/publication/?i=650103.

Gagen, Andrew. "Global Recruiting Trends for 2017." LinkedIn. Accessed August 9, 2020. https://www.linkedin.com/pulse/global-recruiting-trends-2017-andrew-gagen/.

Gentle, Stuart. "The Importance of Social Media in Recruiting." Onrec, September 1, 2017. Accessed August 9, 2020. https://www.onrec.com/news/features/the-importance-of-social-media-in-recruiting.

Guerin, Lisa, J. D. "What Is Progressive Discipline for Employees?" www.nolo.com. Nolo, January 5, 2012. Accessed October 11, 2020. https://www.nolo.com/legal-encyclopedia/employee-progressive-discipline-basics-30242.html.

Imafidon, Casey. "8 Reasons Risk Takers Are More Likely To Be Successful." Landit, September 28, 2019. Accessed November 29, 2020. https://landit.com/articles/8-reasons-risk-takers-are-more-likely-to-be-successful.

Jeanne Mejeur, Michelle Larson-Krieg. "At-Will Employment – Overview." NCLS - National Conference of State Legislatures, April 15, 2008. Accessed October 11, 2020. https://www.ncsl.org/research/labor-and-employment/at-will-employment-overview.aspx.

Jones, Bruce. "Leadership Lessons from Walt Disney: Building Relationships." Disney Institute Blog, Disney, June 12, 2018. Accessed September 13, 2020. https://www.disneyinstitute.com/blog/leadership-lessons-from-walt-disney-building-relationships/.

Knight, Rebecca. "The Right Way to Fire Someone." Harvard Business Review, June 14, 2016. Accessed October 11, 2020. https://hbr.org/2016/02/the-right-way-to-fire-someone.

Lachance-Shandrow, Kim. "How the Color of Your Office Impacts Productivity (Infographic)." Entrepreneur, March 9, 2015. Accessed, November 27, 2020. https://www.entrepreneur.com/article/243749.

Lister, Kate. "Work-at-Home After Covid-19-Our Forecast." Global Workplace Analytics, April 12, 2020. Accessed November 22, 2020. https://globalworkplaceanalytics.com/work-at-home-after-covid-19-our-forecast.

Martin, Rob. "Our Methodology." Great Place to Work®. Accessed November 7, 2020. https://www.greatplacetowork.com/our-methodology.

Martinelli, Katie. "The Importance of Respect in the Workplace: Guide for Managers." The Hub | High Speed Training. High Speed Training, June 10, 2020. Accessed September 21, 2020. https://www.highspeedtraining.co.uk/hub/importance-of-respect-in-the-workplace/.

McFarlane, Sam. "Shared Leadership has Benefits for Everyone." Collective Possibilities, July 10, 2014. Adapted from HBR Blog by Marshall Goldsmith. Accessed September 20, 2020. http://www.collectivepossibilities.com.au/whats-new/shared-leadership-has-benefits-for-everyone/.

Munasinghe, Kate and Gautier Lalith. "Build a Stronger Employee Referral Program." Harvard Business Review, May 26, 2020. Accessed August 9, 2020. https://hbr.org/2020/05/build-a-stronger-employee-referral-program.

Murphy, Kristy. "8 Recruitment Strategies to Attract the Best Talent." Blog, April 3, 2020. Accessed August 9, 2020. https://www.talentlyft.com/en/blog/article/211/8-recruitment-strategies-to-attract-the-best-talent.

O'Dowd, Sean. "Chicago Bulls: Michael Jordan's 10 Best Teammates." Bleacher Report. Bleacher Report, October 3, 2017. Accessed August 16, 2020. https://bleacherreport.com/articles/845166-chicago-bulls-michael-jordans-10-best-teammates.

Roberts, Calia. "Reasons for Immediate Termination." Azcentral.com, September 29, 2016. Accessed October 14, 2020. https://yourbusiness.azcentral.com/reasons-immediate-termination-8026.html.

Robertson, Lee. "Why the Sense of Belonging Is Crucial to Teamwork." AoEC Global, July 18, 2020. Accessed September 13, 2020. https://www.aoec.com/knowledge-bank/why-the-sense-of-belonging-is-crucial-to-teamwork/.

Roth, John. "What Gladiators Can Teach Us About Honor," January 17, 2018. Accessed August 5, 2020. https://goodmenproject.com/featured-content/gladiators-teach-honor-chwm/.

Sauter, Michael B. "The Worst Companies to Work For." 247 Wall St. 24/7 Wall St., January 12, 2020. Accessed September 13, 2020. https://247wallst.com/special-report/2017/06/05/the-worst-companies-to-work-for-3/4/.

Schatz, Traci. "What Makes Teamwork Effective?" Small Business – Chron.com. Chron.com, February 4, 2019. Accessed September 13, 2020. https://smallbusiness.chron.com/teamwork-effective-694.html.

Sherman, Richard M. 1928-. *Walt Disney's The Jungle Book*. Milwaukee, WI: Hal Leonard, 1994.

Somerfield, Claudia. "7 Inspirational Workspace Designs." Work Design Magazine, October 10, 2019. Accessed November 27, 2020. https://www.workdesign.com/2012/02/7-inspirational-workspace-designs/.

Steele, Jeffrey. "How Color Psychology Impacts Today's Workplace." Forbes. Forbes Magazine, January 7, 2020. Accessed, November 27, 2020. https://www.forbes.com/sites/jeffsteele/2020/01/06/how-color-psychology-impacts-todays-workplace/?sh=6d5fb01d10b1.

Stevenson, Mason. "Bad Hiring Costs – By the Numbers." HR Exchange Network. HR Exchange Network, January 10, 2020. Accessed October 10, 2020. https://www.hrexchangenetwork.com/hr-talent-acquisition/articles/poor-hiring-costs-by-the-numbers.

Stratton, Shawn. "5 Tips to Manage the Storming Phase of Group Development." LinkedIn. Accessed October 4, 2020. https://www.linkedin.com/pulse/5-tips-manage-storming-phase-group-development-shawn-stratton.

Trull, Samuel G. "Strategies of Effective Interviewing." Harvard Business Review, August 1, 2014. Accessed August 23, 2020. https://hbr.org/1964/01/strategies-of-effective-interviewing.

Wholley, Meredith. "17 Mind-Blowing Statistics on Performance Reviews and Employee Engagement." ClearCompany, September 10, 2019. Accessed October 13, 2020. https://blog.clearcompany.com/mind-blowing-statistics-performance-reviews-employee-engagement.

About the Author

Louis J. Pepe is the author of three new books, *Reality Based Leadership - Smarter Decision Making*, *Planning for Success*, and *Problem-Solving Today*. He has become a highly respected expert in the world of school finance and operations management based on his ability to strategize, problem-solve, and successfully manage people and resources. His books provide a clear pathway to success with a positive message that is welcomed and needed in navigating today's landscape and tomorrow's challenges. His message is built on inspiration, determination, and reality-based leadership.

He is the president and owner of Lou Pepe Presentations, LLC, consulting on effective management strategies and leadership training through presentations designed for workshops, seminars, conferences, and business meetings.

As a speaker, mentor, and adviser on leadership, operations, and team building, Lou's messages resonate based on his ability to connect with his audiences. As an educator he lives to teach—driven by a mission to inspire others to lead in ways that deliver greater success, satisfaction, and meaning with purpose.

As a key note speaker and presenter, Lou continues to engage audiences across the country with his down-to-earth, practical advice and insights into the everyday challenges in managing people and situations to accomplish organizational goals and objectives.

His blog site, http://businessedissues.blogspot.com/, has gained readership from countries all over the world and featured as "best of blogs" by the American Association of School Administrators.

HONORS AND AWARDS

- School Business Administrator of the Year—New Jersey Association of School Business Officials 2018
- Distinguished Service Award—New Jersey Association of School Business Officials 2018
- Eagle Award 2015 ASBO—Association of School Business Officials International Leadership Achievement Awards
- Pinnacle of Achievement for Innovative Ideas in the field of School Business 2007 ASBO—Association of School Business Officials International
- Oxford Roundtable—2005—Speaker on Issues in Financing Public Education in America, Oxford University, Oxford England.
- Recipient of the US Army Commendation Medal (ARCOM) oak leaf cluster and Achievement Medal

EDUCATION

Pepe earned his bachelor's degree in International Business and Business Administration from Ramapo College of New Jersey and an MBA in Finance from William Paterson University's Christos M. Cotsakos College of Business.

BACKGROUND

He is the assistant superintendent/CFO for the City of Summit Public Schools in Union County, New Jersey, with more than thirty years of leadership experience between military, private, and public service focused on leadership, management, operations, and administration. Prior to entering the field of education, Mr. Pepe was a scanning administrator for the Atlantic & Pacific Tea Company, administrative assistant for SL Industries, and served in the US Army Signal Corps as a tactical signal operator 72E, in Darmstadt, Germany, USAISC as MARS Radio operator at Fort Campbell Kentucky and as an Automated Telecommunications Specialist 72G Shift Supervisor with the 66th Military Intelligence Brigade, Munich, Germany. Through these experiences, Pepe developed leadership skills in team building, management, and communications.

Lou is a past president of the New Jersey Association of School Business Officials, served in community roles to include Councilmen, Board of Education Member and Coach and continues to serve as a mentor for NJ Department of Education State Certification Program. Lou remains connected to Montclair State University as an adjunct professor in the graduate program in education and Saint Peter's University in Jersey City, NJ.

He and his wife live in Lincoln Park, New Jersey, and have two daughters and three grandchildren.

www.ingramcontent.com/pod-product-compliance
Lightning Source LLC
Chambersburg PA
CBHW061332220326
41599CB00026B/5146